Avoid Legal Pitfalls for Small Businesses

Credits

Avoid Legal Pitfalls for Small Businesses

Bevans Solicitors

Hodder Education

338 Euston Road, London NW1 3BH

Hodder Education is an Hachette UK company

First published in UK 2011 by Hodder Education

This edition published 2011

British Library Cataloguing in Publication Data: a catalogue record for this title is available from the British Library.

10 9 8 7 6 5 4 3 2 1

The publisher has used its best endeavours to ensure that any website addresses referred to in this book are correct and active at the time of going to press. However, the publisher and the author have no responsibility for the websites and can make no guarantee that a site will remain live or that the content will remain relevant, decent or appropriate.

The publisher has made every effort to mark as such all words which it believes to be trademarks. The publisher should also like to make it clear that the presence of a word in the book, whether marked or unmarked, in no way affects its legal status as a trademark.

Every reasonable effort has been made by the publisher to trace the copyright holders of material in this book. Any errors or omissions should be notified in writing to the publisher, who will endeavour to rectify the situation for any reprints and future editions.

Hachette UK's policy is to use papers that are natural, renewable and recyclable products and made from wood grown in sustainable forests. The logging and manufacturing processes are expected to conform to the environmental regulations of the country of origin.

www.hoddereducation.co.uk

Typeset by Cenveo Publisher Services

Printed in Great Britain by CPI Cox & Wyman, Reading

Contents

Preface

Any successful business is only as good as its products, services and/or people. We are extremely lucky at Bevans Solicitors to have an excellent team of solicitors based in our Bristol and London offices, all of whom combine outstanding legal knowledge in their specialist field with practical commercial understanding. We are an SME like many of our clients and, therefore, are able not only to advise on pure legal matters but can also bring commercial acumen and guidance to the table from our own experiences.

Particular thanks go to all those who have contributed to this book: Stuart Allen, John Bailey, Alex Bevan, Lucinda Bromfield, Harriet Broughton, John Hodgson, Guy Hollebon, David Kirkpatrick, Lucy Mills, Preema Patel, Filippo Petteni, William Power and Lee Xavier. We must also give a special mention to Jessica Armfelt and Helen Gazzard for their help in pulling the chapters together.

Finally we should point out that the law stated in this book is as at 1 June 2011 and that this book should not be taken as constituting legal advice for a specific issue.

In one minute

In an increasingly regulated business environment there are ever more and ever deeper legal pitfalls for the SME owner or manager. This book seeks to identify a number of common legal pitfalls that SMEs can fall into and provide practical guidance for avoiding them.

Preparation is vital at every stage. For example, even at the earliest stage when planning a business start-up, some careful thought as to the appropriate trading structure – sole trader, partnership, limited liability partnership or limited company – can pay dividends later on. If there are multiple owners, then a basic partnership or shareholder agreement can save significant time, disruption and costs later on when one wants to leave.

As a business becomes established and grows, then new legal pitfalls appear on the horizon. Property issues, staffing issues, debt collection and contracts can all lead to problems, although in the main these can be avoided, or at least the risks can be minimized with some forethought.

Inevitably, there will be problems that arise to which this book does not provide a solution (even we cannot claim that this book will fix all). However, we hope that this book will at least be able to provide a steer to any SME business owner or manager and enable them to identify where a problem may be lying in wait for them. It is then important that practical and commercial advice is sought without delay – depending on the issue, it may be necessary to seek accountancy advice or you may need legal advice. In our experience, it is much better if advice is sought as early as possible because it enables the professional adviser to be proactive and work to avoid the issue developing, rather than having to be reactive since something has already been done and a problem or claim has already crystallized.

1

Setting up a business

In this chapter you will learn about:
- *the different legal forms of business*
- *what steps are necessary to start up your chosen legal structure for your business*
- *shareholders' and partnership agreements and how they can considerably ease the working of your company.*

Initial considerations

When setting up a business, it is extremely important to take time to consider carefully which structure is best suited to the nature of the business itself and the individuals involved and how they intend to carry out that business. From a financial perspective, choosing the correct legal form for your business is key. The legal structure has an effect on:

- ▶ National Insurance and tax liabilities
- ▶ statutory requirements in respect of records/accounts to be kept and filed
- ▶ liability of the business or individuals within the business if the business were to fail
- ▶ the authorities to which the business reports and answers

...and, in more general terms, how the business is run and how decisions are made.

This chapter aims to provide a more detailed overview of the types of legal business structures that exist, their specific characteristics and differences, and their benefits and drawbacks. It is worthwhile carrying out some research online and obtaining as much information as possible from Business Link and Companies House on the types of structure. It is also worth investing in time with a solicitor or accountant to assist in the process of choosing the correct structure that best suits the particular circumstances of the business and individuals concerned. We will take these structures in order.

There are essentially five main choices. These are:

1 sole trader
2 private company (either a private limited or private unlimited company)
3 partnership
4 limited liability partnership
5 public company.

There are also various other business structures that have come into being in more recent times. It should be noted that it is possible to change the legal form of the business after it has commenced trading and has been created, but to effect that change takes time, money, specialist advice (either from accountants in respect of tax implications and/or from solicitors in respect of legal implications) and requires notification to HMRC.

Sole trader

The simplest option is for you to trade on your own behalf and in your own name. Most who start up small businesses find that this is their best option. Though you might well talk about 'your business', as a sole trader in legal terms your business is not an entity that is distinct from you. Your customers and suppliers or anyone with whom you have entered into a contractual relationship in the course of your business will be contracting with you as an individual.

There are upsides and downsides to this structure. All the assets and profits are owned by you but so is the risk. You are personally liable for all debts and liabilities during the course of your business. Many small businesses are structured in this way since the set-up, management, accounting, tax and National Insurance positions are all relatively straightforward. To start up as a sole trader you must simply register with HMRC as being self-employed. Your statutory obligations are to keep accounting records of your business, income and expenses, and to file self-assessment tax returns. All the decisions are yours in respect of the management. You are considered self-employed. You pay fixed-rate Class 2 National Insurance contributions regardless of any profits you make. You pay Class 4 National Insurance contributions on any profit and your profits are taxed as income. You may have to register for VAT depending on the amount of sales. While you have complete control over your business, if you run up debts or if your business does not succeed, any liability lies with you. This will often mean that your home and other assets may be at risk.

POSITIVES

- ▶ You can keep simple, unaudited accounts.
- ▶ National Insurance is low.
- ▶ Unless your earnings are high, you may find that your total tax burden is lower than that of a limited company.
- ▶ Setting up is quick and easy.
- ▶ As your earnings increase, you can form a limited company, although you may have to pay stamp duty to do so.

NEGATIVES

- ▶ You have personal liability for all your business debts. This means that all of your personal assets are at risk.
- ▶ You are entitled to fewer social security benefits.
- ▶ Your options for financing your business are limited.
- ▶ It can be harder to sell your business or pass it on.

Private company

The second structure is that of a private company. There are generally two types of private companies:

1 a private limited company, *and*
2 a private unlimited company (less common).

The great advantage and crucial element of this structure is that, no matter how small or how large the company is, in legal terms it is an entity that is distinct from you. This means that the assets of the company are owned by the company and not by you. If things went wrong, other parties to contracts would sue the company and not you personally. It is the company and not you which has entered into contracts and is liable for all debts and liabilities incurred.

The company is a separate legal entity even if it is entirely and wholly owned by you. There are a number of legal consequences that flow from the separate legal personality of the company. There is a distinction between the assets of a company and your personal assets. The failure of the company, and its possible liquidation, limits the creditors' claim to the assets of the company and not those owned by you.

Some common features of all private companies are that the company must be registered at Companies House, the company must file accounts with Companies House and these accounts should be audited unless they are exempt. A further obligation is to file an annual return with Companies House. There are specific provisions in respect of company secretaries and directors and their eligibility. If the company has any taxable income or profits, there is an obligation to notify HMRC and an obligation to file a corporation tax return. There are a further number of HMRC requirements that must be met – for example, VAT, PAYE, and so on.

A fundamental distinction between a private limited and private unlimited company is that in a limited company the finances are separate from the personal finances of their owner. A company is limited either by shares or by guarantee and, in the event of the company either being wound up or found liable, the members' liability is limited. In reality, there are still many instances when personal liability can still arise, such as in cases of security on borrowings or personal guarantees. In a private unlimited company, there is no limit on liability of its members in the event of the company's liquidation. Such companies are not common and, indeed, it would be unusual to find a small business being a private unlimited company. It is very important in these structures to both have a **shareholders' agreement** (see box below), setting out the relationship between the shareholders and **articles of association**, which define the company structure. The advantages of limited companies tend to increase as the business grows.

POSITIVES

▶ A private limited or unlimited company is a separate entity distinct from you personally.
▶ A limited company carries greater credibility.
▶ It is easier to raise finance for the business or to sell a part of the business.

► High earners can gain tax advantages either by keeping money in the business or making dividend or pension payments.

NEGATIVES

► There is a great deal of red tape associated with registering a limited company (although your solicitor or accountant may be able to make life easier here by buying an 'off-the-shelf' company on your behalf, or you can use a reputable company registration agent) and appointing directors.
► Annual accounts are generally more complex.
► Companies with turnovers of greater than £6.5 million require an independent audit, with all of the associated costs and administration.
► National Insurance payments are higher, given the requirement to pay employer's and employee's NI contributions on all salaries, including those of the company directors.
► If you decide to cease trading, it can be more difficult and more expensive to wind up your company.

Shareholders' agreements

At law a company is a separate legal entity and quite distinct from its shareholders (the owners), the directors (who run the company day to day) and the employees. It may be that an individual is a shareholder, director and employee, but one of the core strengths of the limited company vehicle is the fact that there can be a separation of ownership from management. It is therefore very important that the owners' – the shareholders' – rights, duties, obligations and powers are clearly set out. The articles of association of the company may provide a basic framework; however, normally the articles of association will not cover all of the important matters such as how a shareholder can transfer their shares if they leave. Moreover, the articles of association are public documents which must be filed with Companies House and so anyone can obtain a copy. Ordinarily, the shareholders will not want the details of their arrangements available publicly and so will opt for a shareholders' agreement which will be private as between them and which will govern their relationships as shareholders.

A shareholders' agreement must be tailored to the particular business, and you should always seek legal advice before entering into such an important document. Further, the shareholders' agreement should be a living document in the sense that it should grow with your business. There is little point incurring the cost of having a 100-page, all singing, all dancing agreement drawn up from day one if the business is a new start-up and costs are tight. In this scenario, a basic well-drafted agreement would provide the core protections necessary, and over time, as the business grows, the agreement can be redrafted to become more sophisticated. A shareholders' agreement is particularly important if there are minority shareholders as the agreement will be a chance for them to ensure appropriate protection of their minority interests in the company, although much will depend on their relative negotiating strength as to how much protection they can obtain.

Common things that ought to be considered and dealt with in a shareholders' agreement include:

► *Whether there are any core business decisions that require unanimity of all the shareholders.* Under company law, most company decisions require a simple majority of the shareholders and so 51 per cent of the vote suffices. There are some matters which require 75 per cent of the votes but nothing requires unanimity. Therefore, a shareholders' agreement will commonly set out certain important decisions that can only be taken with the written agreement of all shareholders. These typically include:
  ▷ the selling, transferring, leasing, assigning or otherwise disposing of a material part of, or any interest in, the undertaking, property or assets of the company or any subsidiary
  ▷ doing anything whereby the company may be wound up (whether voluntarily or compulsorily) unless the company is insolvent

▷ entering into any contract except in the ordinary and proper course of business
▷ borrowing money
▷ taking major decisions relating to the conduct of material legal proceedings to which the company is a party
▷ incurring capital expenditure above a certain limit
▷ holding any meeting of shareholders unless all shareholders or duly authorized representatives or proxies for each of the shareholders are present
▷ amending the articles of association of the company
▷ altering any rights or restrictions attached to any class of shares
▷ changing the company's name
▷ passing any resolution or engaging in any other matter which represents a substantial change in the nature of the company's business or in the manner in which that business is conducted
▷ removing a director
▷ issuing any additional shares otherwise than in accordance with the shareholders' agreement.

▶ *Whether a shareholder has the right to be a director* (or to appoint a director to represent their interests).
▶ *Any policy on dividend payments.* It may be that dividends will simply be declared as and when there are funds and appropriate company approval is given, or there may be an express dividend policy – for example, that a certain percentage of profit will be paid as a dividend each year.
▶ *A requirement that a shareholder who wishes to transfer shares to a third party to first offer the shares for sale to the other shareholders.* This ensures that the shareholders will not end up in business with people whom they do not know or do not want to be in business with. Typically, there will be a fixed procedure to be followed if a shareholder wishes to transfer shares. It will need to be determined

whether the remaining shareholders have an option to buy the outgoing shareholders' shares and, if they do not exercise the option, then the shares can be transferred to the third party, or whether it is an obligation on the remaining shareholders to buy the shares. The amount to be paid for the shares will have to be worked out – typically, a shareholders' agreement will provide for the parties to try and agree the figure first and, if not, then such amount is to be determined by an independent accountant. There may need to be a mechanism to deal with the situation where the parties cannot even agree on the accountant who is to undertake the valuation! The shareholders' agreement should also provide a framework for how to calculate the share value – including whether there will be a discount for a minority shareholding, what valuation mechanism will be used, and so on. The remaining share-holders may want to allow for payment over a period of time.

▶ *Whether there are situations which trigger an automatic transfer of shares.* These events are commonly insolvency or death of a shareholder. In addition, where a shareholder is an employee as well, then the termination of their employment (whether by the company or a resignation) would often trigger an automatic transfer of the shares, as would a breach of the shareholders' agreement itself. It may be that there will be good leaver/bad leaver provisions, so that, for example, a shareholder employee who is made redundant through no fault of their own is paid full value for the shares whereas a shareholder employee who is dismissed by the company because of misconduct may be paid only a nominal amount for the shares.

▶ *Drag and tag rights.* These would apply where a majority shareholder wishes to sell their shareholding. In this scenario, the third-party purchaser may want to acquire the entire shareholding of the company and not just the majority of the shares, or the minority shareholder(s) face being in business with someone they do not know and may not be comfortable with. In order to avoid this, then the shareholders' agreement can provide that, if the majority shareholder receives an offer from a third party for all of the shares in the company, then the minority shareholder(s) must sell to the third party on the same terms as the majority shareholder is selling (drag rights). Alternatively, if the third party offers to buy all or some of the majority shareholders' shares, only then can the minority insist that the third party must also purchase all or the same proportion of their shares on the same terms (tag rights).

▶ *Either a full prohibition on issuing new shares at all* (i.e. this is a decision that requires unanimity of the shareholders) or, alternatively, if the company intends to issue new shares, *a provision they must first be offered pro rata to the existing shareholders.* This ensures that new shares cannot be issued with the effect of watering down an individual's shareholding and so, in turn, their voting rights.

▶ *Possible restrictions on the future activity of the departing shareholder* – for example, that they must not solicit, canvass or deal with customers/clients of the company, or that they must not hold an interest in a competing business for a specific period of time. Such restrictions require very careful drafting to minimize the risk that a court declares them unenforceable.

▶ *A dispute resolution clause.* Ordinarily, a dispute about shareholding matters would end up in the civil courts and so there would be a public hearing which might involve confidential and private business matters. It is therefore sensible to think about including a clause so that any dispute which arises between the shareholders must first be referred to, say, mediation. See Chapter 8 for details of mediation.

Partnership

If more than one person is involved in running the structure of the business, a third possible structure is that of a partnership. The three types of partnership are:

1 limited partnerships
2 ordinary partnerships (which incorporate the general characteristics outlined below), *and*
3 limited liability partnerships, or LLPs (considered separately below).

However, there are some features common to all three types of partnership. Each partner must register as self-employed with HMRC and complete an annual self-assessment tax return. A partner can be a business or an individual. The partners share risks, responsibilities and costs of the business. Unless stated otherwise in a **partnership agreement** (see box below), each partner will take an equal share of profits. It is normal for the partners themselves to manage and run the business. The partnership has obligations to send annual returns to HMRC and keep details of business transactions, income and expenses. It is they who enter into the agreement with third parties and are therefore liable for all debts and liabilities incurred in the course of the business. A partnership, unlike a private company, is not a separate legal entity. Serious consideration should be given to drawing up a partnership agreement. In practice, it is essential.

POSITIVES AND NEGATIVES

Positives and negatives are similar to those of a sole trader. The following should be considered:

▶ Your partnership may be able to accrue additional finance via the introduction of new partners.
▶ Each partner is personally liable for all the business debts of the partnership (other than tax on profits), even if another partner caused them.
▶ Partnership agreements can be established to protect the partnership in the event of any disputes. You should consult your lawyer about this.

Limited partnerships are partnerships where at least one partner has unlimited liability (general partner) and one or more partners have limited liability (limited partners) provided they take no part in the running of the business. This form is used sometimes for investment funds or for joint ventures between companies.

Partnership agreements

A partnership involves two or more people running a business with a view to profit. Inevitably, those involved in a partnership will have different objectives for the business and different timescales within which they wish to achieve those objectives. A partnership agreement will regulate the way in which the partners act towards each other and will set out the rules for the partnership. In the absence of a formal written partnership agreement, the partnership will be governed by the Partnership Act 1890.

A partnership agreement should be a living document in the sense that it should grow with your business. As with a shareholders' agreement, if the business is a new start-up and costs are tight, a basic, well-drafted agreement will provide the core protections necessary; then, over time, as the business grows, the agreement can be redrafted to become more sophisticated.

Common things that ought to be considered and dealt with in a partnership agreement include:

▶ *Who the partners are*. This may sound obvious, but if somebody is investing in a partnership business through their own limited company, is the intention that the limited company will be a partner? Are there any 'sleeping partners' who may not have day-to-day involvement in the business but who have contributed capital? Are they partners or have they provided a loan to the partnership?
▶ *When the partnership commenced*. Often there can be a dispute about the date the partnership started, especially if a large transaction was completed at around that time; was the profit from the deal part

of the partnership to be split equally or was it a deal done by an individual before the partnership commenced and so the profit is for that individual only? Are there any earlier contracts or agreements between the partners which need to be formally cancelled or ratified?

▶ *What the business will actually do.* Will it have the freedom to undertake other types of work or will this need the agreement of the partners?

▶ *How long the partnership is expected to last.* Will it continue indefinitely or is it to continue for a fixed period of time or until a fixed event has occurred? Under the Partnership Act, certain events trigger a dissolution or termination of a partnership such as death or bankruptcy of a partner. The partnership agreement can exclude these events from causing an automatic termination of the partnership. By doing this, you will avoid the formality, in the event of death or bankruptcy of a partner, of having to wind up the partnership business and then form a new partnership with the continuing partners who acquired the business from the old partnership. It is commonplace for a partnership agreement to provide that death or bankruptcy ends that partner's involvement in the partnership (which may trigger payments to the deceased or bankrupt partner) but does not terminate the entire partnership.

▶ *The name of the partnership.* Does the name comply with the Business Names Act 1985? Are there any professional restrictions on the choice of name?

▶ *Where the business will operate from.* Is there a freehold or leasehold interest? Are the premises part of the partnership assets (and therefore owned in the proportion of partnership shares) or are they owned outside of the partnership, with the partnership business paying rent to occupy them. Is all the property to be used by the partnership (e.g. computer equipment, machines, tools, etc.) to be partnership property or will all or part of the equipment be owned individually by one or more partners? If the latter, on what basis can the partnership use those assets? Is any rent or hire charge to be made?

▶ *Whether the business uses any intellectual property.* If so, who owns the intellectual property rights – is this a partnership asset?

▶ *Any specific requirements about what books of account should be kept and how frequently accounts should be produced.* Are there any restrictions on partners' rights to access the financial records of the business and/or receive accounts? Do the accounts need to be signed by all partners, or, if one refuses, can the others approve the accounts?

▶ *The bank that the business will use.* Who are the cheque signatories and/or are on the bank mandate?

▶ *The initial capital that each partner contributes.* This will regulate what share of the business each partner owns. If non-monetary contributions are to be made, then how will this be valued? Should there be a power to make a call for further capital? (For example, one possible stipulation might be that, if 75 per cent of the partners agree, then all the partners must contribute additional funds.) Is interest to be payable on any repayment of capital? If so, at what rate and when (will it be paid monthly or annually during the existence of the partnership, or will it only be paid when capital is repaid)?

▶ *Whether the partnership will pay the tax of the partners.* If so, what reserves are to be made for this? Will there be a full payment annually of any current account balances, or will any undrawn current account sums be transferred to the capital accounts at year-end?

▶ *The level of drawings which the partners can take.* What happens if there are cash pressures on the business – can the level of drawings be reduced? Does this require consent of all partners or simply a majority?

▶ *How the profits are to be shared.* Are the shares fixed, or is a more sophisticated model to be used so that profit share increases over time and/or is dependent on a partner's performance. Are there any salaried or fixed-share partners who get paid a prior salary or fixed amount out of the profits before they are distributed to the other equity partners? What happens if a partner is away from the business with good reason (for example, because of ill health, sabbatical or maternity/paternity/adoption leave)? Will they continue to receive their profit share? What if there is no authorization to be absent? Should the business insure against a partner being absent for ill health to fund ongoing profit-share payments?

▶ *Whether the partners are to work full-time in the business* – this is usually stated to be devoting full-time attention to the business – or whether some or all will work part-time.

▶ *How often partners' meetings will be held.* What are the notice requirements for convening a partners' meeting? Are any key matters to be decided by unanimity? What percentage of vote suffices to pass a resolution? What happens if there is a deadlock? (Does the chair have a casting vote, should an independent person be appointed to determine the way forward, does the decision just not get passed?) Will there be a managing partner and/or senior partner? What are the responsibilities and authority levels for those roles and how are appointments to be made? Is there to be a management committee and, if so, what authority does the committee have?

▶ *Are there to be any limits on a partner's authority to bind the partnership?*

▶ *The amount of holiday that each partner can take.* Are there any restrictions on when it can be taken? Can untaken holiday be carried over to the next year, or is it a 'use it or lose it' system?

▶ *How a partner can leave the partnership.* What notice of such retirement must be given? Can it be given at any time or are there limits (for example, no retirement in the first three years of the business starting up).

▶ *Whether a partner can be forced to leave (expelled) from the partnership.* If so, in what circumstances? What procedure must be followed before expulsion?

▶ *Whether the partnership has the right to suspend a partner pending an investigation into any problems.* What is the suspension procedure? Can the partnership require a partner who has given notice of retirement not to undertake work (i.e., put them on 'garden leave')?

▶ *Where a partner is leaving the partnership, how their share of the business is to be valued.* In particular, what will be the position in respect of goodwill and work in progress? What happens if the value cannot be agreed by the partners – who determines the final figures?

▶ *Whether the remaining partners have an option to acquire the outgoing partner's share or whether they have an obligation to do so.* What are the time limits for exercising such an option? Are payments to be made in one go, or are they to be spread over a period of time, and, if the latter, what period, and will interest accrue on the unpaid balance, and at what rate?

▶ *Whether there are to be any restrictions on an outgoing partner* – for example, restrictive covenants preventing the outgoing partner soliciting, canvassing or dealing with the partnership's customers or clients, or a non-compete clause.

▶ *Finally, and perhaps most critically, what happens if there is a dispute.* Ordinarily, any partnership dispute would be determined by the courts and this can be a costly process. Should there be provision for alternative dispute resolution, such as mediation, to try and resolve a dispute quickly and confidentially (See Chapter 8 for more details on mediation.)

Limited liability partnership

Under the Limited Liability Partnerships Act 2000, a new form of business entity was created – the 'LLP'. This is essentially a mix between a partnership and a limited company and it aims to combine the lack of formality of partnerships together with the limitation in liability of a limited company. Since introduction of the 2000 Act, the majority of businesses that have become LLPs started off as partnerships and the change has been principally motivated by a desire to limit the liability of the partners.

In summary, an LLP...

- ▶ is a corporate body with its own legal identity and capacity
- ▶ has the organizational flexibility of a partnership
- ▶ is taxed as a partnership – tax is charged on all the profits, whether or not they are distributed to members
- ▶ must prepare and file annual accounts and comply with other filing requirements at Companies House
- ▶ may claw back partnership withdrawals up to two years after it has been declared insolvent, *and*
- ▶ can be regulated via a members' agreement, which is something of a cross between a shareholders' agreement and a partnership agreement in much the same way that an LLP is a hybrid between the partnership model and the limited company vehicle.

Public company

A further form of company is the public limited company. It is unlikely that a small business user will create this form of company, but it may come across them in its dealings. Public limited companies, or PLCs, exist in their own right. As in the case of limited companies, their finances are separate from the personal finances of their members. They have particular requirements in their set-up. Whether a company is a private or a public limited company depends essentially on its constitution. A PLC must have shares issued to the public of a share value of £50,000 or the equivalent in euros. It must be incorporated at Companies House, have at least two directors and shareholders, and have a qualified company secretary. The company's constitution must state that it is a public company and include the words 'public limited company' or 'PLC'. Any company which does not qualify as a public limited company is a private company. PLCs can be financed by the selling of shares to the general public or to other companies. Their shareholding may be listed on the Stock Exchange or the Alternative Investment Market. A price will be quoted at which dealings with the company's shares should occur.

The PLC must file yearly audited accounts (unless specified) with Companies House as well as an annual return. Profits and income generated by the PLC are liable to corporation tax and a company tax return must be filed. In respect of the shareholders, profits are normally distributed as dividends. As with limited companies, members are not responsible for the company's debts unless they have given guarantees and the liability of each member is limited to the unpaid amount on their shares.

Other business structures

European economic interest groupings, European companies, community interest companies and charitable incorporated organizations are other forms that businesses can take. We will not go into detail about their structure as it is unlikely that a small business would be interested in these forms of company. However, it is worth noting that charitable incorporated organizations were introduced pursuant to the Charities Act 2006 as a new legal form of incorporation designed specifically for charities. The idea behind this form of company was to provide a corporate structure that avoided the duplication involved in charities having to report both to the Charity Commission and Companies House.

Conclusion

In summary, the key differences between a company whether private or public and a sole trader or partnership is that the company has a distinct legal personality from its members and a limitation of their liability. These factors encourage business entrepreneurship. The existence of a company may also give some security to those trading with it in that the records filed with Companies House showing the structure and accounts of the company are obtainable, giving an insight into its financial position. Recent legislation in the Companies Act 2006 has sought to consolidate, streamline and clarify – using predominantly non-technical legal language – the structure and operations of companies, and has legislated in respect of directors, secretaries, meetings, accounting, shares and share capital, articles of association, formation, and so on.

As we have seen, there is a significant variety in the business structures that are available to a small business. Each form has positives and negatives; it is worth getting this right by spending thought and effort in looking at the business structure at its start.

TEST YOURSELF

1 You need to register a sole trader business with Companies House. True or false?

2 A sole trader can operate as...

 (a) any type of business

 (b) a shoe shop

 (c) a fishmonger

3 A limited company has...

 (a) a limited time to trade until it is automatically wound up

 (b) limited liability for the shareholders

 (c) a limit on the number of directors

4 A partner is liable...

 (a) jointly and severally for all debts of the business

 (b) for an equal proportion of the debts of the business

 (c) for nothing at all

 (d) for £1 only

5 An LLP is...

 (a) a likeable laughing partner

 (b) a limited liability partnership

 (c) an old type of record

 (d) something you should consult your doctor about

6 You cannot change the structure of your business once you have been trading for more than two years. True or false?

7 An LLP must file accounts with Companies House?

 (a) yes

 (b) no

 (c) maybe

 (d) not got a clue

2

....

Property

In this chapter you will learn about:
- *considerations you should take when negotiating and entering into a new business lease*
- *responsibilities for leasehold repairs*
- *environmental issues, especially with regard to contaminated land*
- *stamp duty land tax.*

Entering into a new business lease

When entering into a lease, in addition to the rent or the premium you are paying, you are entering into long-running obligations to your landlord which are potentially extremely onerous. If these matters are not addressed when negotiating the lease, it may be difficult to alter them at a later stage.

TERM

You should try not to agree a lease with a **term** (i.e. the length) which is longer than you expect to need the property for.

If you are likely to want the property for a long time, a longer lease may be better and you may be able to push the rent down as a result. However, you should also bear in mind that you need not necessarily agree a long term simply to be able to stay at the property (i.e. to be contracted in under the Landlord and Tenant Act and having the ability to obtain a renewal of the term).

If the landlord wants a longer lease than you want, it may be possible to agree that you have the right to terminate the lease at the end of some specified period of the lease (e.g. a ten-year lease but with the tenant's right to break the lease at the end of the fifth year). Normally, three to six months' notice will need to be given to break the term. It is possible to have a 'mutual landlord and tenant break clause' allowing either party to break or a 'landlord or tenant only break clause'. A 'tenant only break clause' is preferable.

RENT

Is the proposed rent realistic? You can either approach another commercial agent for his/her view or you can look at other similar properties to see if the rent is similar. You need to remember that the agent will have put in the highest figure and therefore the figure may be negotiable. You also need to remember this if you are comparing the rent with other advertised rents.

If the lease is not 'full repairing and insuring' (see below), there will be an increase in the rent to provide the landlord with funds to do repairs.

INSURANCE AND REPAIRS

The landlord will usually want to agree terms on what is known as a **'full repairing and insuring'** basis. This means that on top of the rent the tenant will pay the premium for insuring the building and will be responsible for all repairs. If you are taking a short lease (e.g. less than ten years), this may not be appropriate.

The repairing obligation usually requires you to keep the property in good repair and to hand it back at the end of the lease in good repair. This represents a substantial liability, particularly on other than new properties.

If you take a property which is not in good repair and on the basis of 'full repairing', you will find yourself – either during the lease or at the end – required by the landlord to put it in repair or to pay for the cost of such repair. This can be very expensive and you should consider:

- ▶ requiring the landlord to do the necessary works to put the property in repair before you take the lease
- ▶ agreeing a rent-free period to compensate for the cost of putting the property in good repair
- ▶ making the 'full repairing' basis subject to a **schedule of condition** – a report which records the state of repair at the date

of commencement and obliges you to leave the property in no better state of repair, *or*

▶ seeking to limit the repairing obligation to internal repair only.

A fuller explanation of leasehold repairs is detailed in the next section of this chapter.

RENT REVIEWS

A **rent review** is the right for the landlord to call for the rent to be varied at some time during the lease. The rent is based usually on market rents for similar properties at the time of the review.

Landlords almost always seek an 'upwards only' review, which means that, if market rents have fallen, the old rent continues rather than goes down. Rarely can a landlord be persuaded to accept a rent review clause going either way.

SERVICE CHARGES

If you are taking a part of a building, there may be a **service charge** in addition to the rent. The service charge covers the cost of the landlord repairing the exterior and structure thereby making the lease effectively 'full repairing'.

The service charge may cover a large number of costs (e.g. cleaning common parts, landscaping, security, etc) and the landlord may not be too cost-conscious, as he/she knows he/she can pass the costs on to the tenants.

You need to establish:

▶ what percentage of the total costs will be charged to your lease and how this figure has been calculated
▶ what services are provided
▶ what actual cost has the service charge been in the last three years and are there any additional large service charge items envisaged for the future (e.g. roof replacement), *and*
▶ whether the total service charge can be capped.

COSTS

You may be asked to pay the landlord's solicitor's costs for granting the lease. This should be resisted, but, if the landlord insists, then you should only agree to pay a maximum contribution to the landlord's costs.

Responsibilities for leasehold repairs

One of the most common areas of dispute between landlords and tenants is that of repair – namely, who should be responsible and to what standard. Mistakes when a lease is entered into can prove very costly both during the lease and when it comes to an end.

On the grant of a lease, certain covenants are implied. These are:

▶ The tenant is under a duty to use the premises in a tenant-like manner.
▶ The landlord may be held liable if he/she fails to maintain the common parts of a building (e.g. the stairs, hallways, lifts, etc.).
▶ The landlord may be under an implied obligation to repair so as to give business efficacy to the lease (e.g. if the tenant is responsible for the interior it can be implied that the landlord is responsible for the outside).

In practical terms, the above cover very few of the problems which can arise and so it is important that repairing obligations are clearly set out in the lease. Those obligations will depend greatly on the length of the lease, the type of building and, of course, the bargaining position of the parties involved.

TYPES OF REPAIRING OBLIGATIONS

Most landlords will ideally be looking to grant a **'full repairing lease'**, which in simple terms means that he/she will be under no obligation to repair. Any rent received will be profit and the tenant will be required to return the premises to the landlord at the end of the term in a good state of repair (which could be better than the condition when the tenant first entered into the lease).

If the premises are part of a large building rented as individual units by different tenants, the landlord will usually deal with repairs by way of a service charge. Each tenant will pay a proportion of the costs of repair of the whole building (including those common parts which are not let), and again the rent received by the landlord is profit. The tenant will, of course, still be responsible for keeping the internal areas in repair.

Some landlords will be happy to pay for repairs from the rent received. An example of this would be where the landlord occupies most of the building and is responsible for repairs in any event and so is not too concerned about contributions from a tenant of a small part. Again the tenant should usually expect to be responsible for internal repairs.

VARYING REPAIRING OBLIGATIONS

The different types of obligations referred to above are only a starting point. There are a number of variations that can be made. For example:

▶ The lease can exclude the tenant from any responsibility for inherent defects such as those caused by a poor design or the use of substandard materials. This obligation should then be passed on to the landlord who may have more knowledge of the premises and so is more comfortable with accepting the risk.

▶ The landlord will usually insure the building against a number of risks. The tenant should look carefully at the list to see that it covers foreseeable eventualities and then seek confirmation that the landlord will not look to him/her to carry out repairs which are insured against.

▶ The tenant should as a matter of course have a survey of the property carried out to reveal any future problems. If the survey reveals problems which the tenant can live with without repairing, he/she could request that a schedule of condition is inserted into the lease. This will give a condition at the commencement of the lease as a yardstick to compare the condition at the end. The tenant will be under no obligation to leave the premises at the end of the lease in a better condition than it was at the commencement of the lease.

▶ If the repairs need to be carried out before the tenant can trade, he/she can ask for a rent-free period. This will mean that, instead of paying rent for the first few months, the tenant can spend the money carrying out repairs.

WHAT HAPPENS AT THE END OF THE LEASE?

At the end of a full repairing lease the tenant will be required to 'yield up in repair'. As mentioned above, this may be a better state of repair than at the start of the lease.

In other types of lease (not full repairing), the obligations will vary according to the exact terms of the lease. Most leases will, however, require the tenant to redecorate to the landlord's satisfaction.

Normally, the issue of repairs at the end of the lease will involve the landlord preparing a **schedule of dilapidations** recording the items of disrepair for which he/she considers the tenant to be liable under the terms of the lease. Often the tenant may choose to instruct a surveyor to look at the lease and negotiate with the landlord to agree what repairs are to be carried out by the tenant.

Control of asbestos at the workplace

Most businesses may not be particularly concerned as to whether or not their buildings contain asbestos. However, the issue is becoming one of importance not just for all employers but for all occupiers of non-residential property.

Regulation 4 of the Control of Asbestos at Work Regulations 2002 requires owners or others with responsibility for maintaining and repairing non-residential properties, or controlling access to those properties, to manage the risk from asbestos. Although asbestos is not harmful until it disintegrates or is removed, 'duty holders' must:

▶ take reasonable steps to identify asbestos within their premises, the amount present and its condition
▶ presume that materials do contain asbestos (e.g. in areas that are not easily accessible) unless there is strong evidence to the contrary
▶ make and keep an up-to-date record of the location and condition of the asbestos/presumed asbestos
▶ undertake a risk assessment and prepare a plan to manage those risks
▶ implement a risk-management plan and to provide information on the asbestos-containing materials to those likely to encounter it (e.g. maintenance contractors and the emergency services)
▶ undertake ongoing monitoring.

The sight of an asbestos report seems a sensible prerequisite before taking on any lease.

Environmental issues

Are you thinking of buying or renting some land or property? Do you know whether the land or property is contaminated? Are you aware of your potential responsibilities for cleaning up contaminated land? Are you making a very expensive mistake?

WHAT IS CONTAMINATED LAND?

The Contaminated Land regime came into force on 1 April 2000 and the legislation lays down a complex formula for deciding whether the land is contaminated or not. The local authority (which is the 'enforcing authority' for the land) has to be satisfied that significant harm is being caused, or there is significant possibility of such harm being caused or pollution of controlled waters is being or is likely to be caused.

Harm is regarded as significant only if it is of the following types:

▶ death, disease, serious injury, etc., to human beings
▶ irreversible adverse change in the ecological system
▶ death, disease or damage to animals and crops, *or*
▶ damage to buildings.

If the local authority is satisfied that the land is contaminated, they can serve a notice on those responsible requiring them to clean it up. Such a notice is called a **remediation notice**.

WHO PAYS FOR REMEDIATION?

Government policy is that the polluter should pay. All or any of the (possibly several) persons who have contributed to the pollution should bear the cost of resolving the problems which it has caused.

Under the regulations, there are three parties who may become responsible for the clean-up operation:

1 the person(s) who caused or knowingly permitted the pollution (see below)
2 the owner for the time being of the contaminated land
3 the occupier for the time being of the contaminated land.

Who is responsible?

'Permitting' the pollution can consist of merely allowing the pollution to occur (i.e. not preventing it if it was possible to do so). It also covers allowing the pollution to remain on a site even if it was already there when the site was bought. Failing to remove such pollution may make a person liable as the original polluter of the site.

A person is only responsible if they 'knowingly' permitted the pollution to occur. There is a view that, in addition to actual knowledge of the circumstances, turning a blind eye or failing to make any enquiries may attract liability. If a site owner or purchaser could have found out about the contamination (e.g. by survey or investigation), and could have done something to stop or remove it but failed to take those steps, they may be said to have 'knowingly' permitted it, and may become liable as the original polluter to receive a remediation notice.

Where the local authority cannot find the original polluter, the owner or occupier for the time being becomes liable to clean up the land.

EXCLUDED PERSONS

The regulations lay down special circumstances in which a party who would normally be liable for the clean-up operation can avoid liability (e.g. anyone who makes a relevant payment for the clean-up of land or anyone who has sold land having provided sufficient information to the buyer to enable them to be aware of the pollution risk).

IMPLICATIONS FOR PROPERTY TRANSACTIONS

In any transaction involving the purchase or leasing of property, the main concerns are that:

▶ a costly environmental liability may be inherited by the buyer, *and*
▶ the value of the property or site may be substantially reduced, even to the point of being unsaleable, as a consequence of contamination within the site or neighbouring property.

It is not always the polluter who pays but occasionally the current owner or occupier, so buyers and tenants have to be vigilant and would be advised to carry out various steps which may include any or all of the following:

▶ making full enquiries of the seller, asking for details of any pollution incidents or accidents affecting the site; details of previous owners or occupiers and activities carried on by them; and whether the seller is aware of any potential contamination on the site or neighbouring sites
▶ making full searches of any public registers regarding the site and adjacent land
▶ undertaking an independent site history investigation by obtaining a site investigation report from a commercial search company
▶ initiating a full site investigation by environmental consultants including a soil survey
▶ obtaining a contractual indemnity from the seller against the costs.
▶ agreeing a reduction in the price to cover the cost of the clean-up operation or to take into account the reduction in value
▶ obtaining insurance cover against the risks of liability resulting from contamination (although such premiums are likely to be expensive).

Stamp duty land tax

If you are purchasing the freehold of a property or taking on a lease, it is important to be aware of the significant financial impact that **stamp duty land tax** (SDLT) may have on your transaction.

A DIFFERENT APPROACH

Broadly, SDLT will have an impact on a transaction when it has been completed or when it has been 'substantially completed'. Substantial completion is tested by such elements as payment of all or the vast proportion of the purchase price and whether possession has been given to the purchasers. This needs to be carefully reviewed because of the fines to be levied for late notification.

RATES OF DUTY

Rates of duty for purchase prices and lease premiums where the property is not in a disadvantaged area are (at the time of writing):

Property value	Rate of duty
£0–£150,000	0%
£150,001–£250,000	1%
£250,001–£500,000	3%
Over £500,000	4%

For leases, SDLT is charged at 1 per cent of the **Net Present Value** (NPV) of rent throughout the term of the lease. Generally, this is calculated as the actual rent payable in the first five years of the lease (any review of rent in the five-year period that is not capable of calculation being ignored) and a rent for any period of the lease after five years being assumed to be the highest rent calculable for any year in the first five years.

SDLT on VAT is only charged if VAT is actually being paid on the rent rather than being assumed as being paid on any lease where there is provision for VAT to be charged.

There is a discount, however, of 3.5 per cent per annum on the rents calculated cumulatively year on year. The calculation is very complicated – fortunately, there is a calculator on the HMRC website at www.hmrc.gov.uk/so/sdlt/calculate/calculators.htm#2

SDLT is chargeable at 1 per cent on the excess of the NPV over £150,000 for commercial properties.

WHAT IS CHARGEABLE?

While standard purchases of freehold and grants and assignments of leases are clearly covered by the definition of 'acquisition', the definition itself is much greater being the 'creation, surrender, release or variation of a chargeable interest', and a 'chargeable interest' includes 'any freehold or leasehold rights over another's land (e.g. easements, etc.) and powers of appointment in trusts'. Every acquisition of an interest in land is chargeable to SDLT unless it is exempt.

EXEMPT INTERESTS

Certain interests in land are exempt from SDLT. These include mortgages and personal licences to use and occupy land and tenancies at will. Exempt transactions do not require notification of any sort.

EXEMPT AND RELIEF TRANSACTIONS

These are transactions either falling within a list, the most common of which are set out below, or are for no consideration. The list of exempt transactions includes gifts, dispositions under wills or intestacy or to beneficiaries under a trust, certain transactions on the ending of a marriage or following a person's death.

Consideration (discussed in more detail in Chapter 5) can be a cash amount but can include non-monetary items such as the release or assumption of a debt, work or services and/or the transfer of other property. Non-monetary consideration will be valued at fair market value.

In disadvantaged areas of the country, relief applies to residential or mixed-use properties where the consideration is £150,000 or less. The exact requirements are covered on the HMRC website.

NOTIFICATION

Transactions needing notification must be notified to HMRC and SDLT paid within 30 days of the date of the transaction taking place (rather than the date of the documentation that may evidence it).

Full notification is required in relation to any land transaction requiring notification (i.e. not an exempt interest or an exempt transfer), even though the consideration is below the statutory thresholds. Additionally, full notification is also required if the transaction qualifies not for exemption but relief. There is a long list of reliefs – the most common in practice are likely to be designated disadvantaged areas, chain-breaking purchasing companies, and company group and reconstruction relief.

Also of importance in practice is that structured sale agreements, which provided some relief on exchanges of land, have been ended so each will be regarded separately and charged to SDLT in full.

Failure to notify within the prescribed time and pay SDLT attracts an immediate automatic fine of £100 with a further £100 fine three months later.

The notification is in very similar form to a tax return and, indeed, that is exactly what it is. HMRC has also indicated it will carry out spot checks and make enquiries of tax payers and has six years from the date of the transaction to do so.

TEST YOURSELF

1 A lease is...

   (a) a legally binding agreement to rent premises

   (b) the first stage of purchasing an office block

   (c) nothing to worry about

   (d) 'A-lease, A-lease, who the hell is A-lease?'

2 In order to bring a lease to an end you must...

   (a) serve three months' notice at any time

   (b) comply with the terms of the lease as to when notice may be served

   (c) do nothing and wait for the expiry of the term

   (d) scarper under cover of darkness leaving no forwarding address and significant rent arrears

3 You are a landlord and do not want to have to pay the costs of repairing the building. You should ensure that you get a lease with your tenant which is...

   (a) fully repairing and insuring

   (b) fully comp

   (c) half-cut

   (d) half-baked

4 In order to avoid liability for environmental damage as a tenant you should...

   (a) undertake appropriate searches and checks before entering into the lease

   (b) blame someone else for any pollution

   (c) chuck your waste products over the fence as you never liked the bloke that owns the business next door

   (d) seek new indemnities from the Environment Agency

3

Intellectual property explained

In this chapter you will learn about:
- *the different types of intellectual property rights*
- *how such rights may be infringed and defences and remedies for infringement.*

Introduction

The value of **intellectual property** (IP) can be underestimated and, if not protected properly, it may put your business at risk. A basic understanding of the law will allow you to understand the mechanisms that allow you to protect what you create, maximize your competitive position and avoid infringing the IP rights of other people and businesses.

In this chapter, we will provide an introduction to trade marks, copyright and patents; how these rights might be found to infringe others' rights or how they might be infringing your rights; and defences and remedies to infringement.

Types of intellectual property rights

IP rights fall into two general categories:

1 **Registered rights** – granted on application to the UK Intellectual Property Office. However, even if granted, their validity can be challenged. Registered rights are monopoly rights, which means that, once registered, the owner can stop others from using the right without permission. Registered rights include patents, trade marks and registered designs.

2 Unregistered rights – these arise automatically, give protection against copying or using the right, and include copyright, unregistered design rights, rights in unregistered trade marks and confidential information.

Patents

WHAT IS PROTECTED?

Patents protect most industrially applicable processes and devices, including:

- ▶ mechanical devices (e.g. a vacuum cleaner)
- ▶ methods for doing things (e.g. a method for printing textiles)
- ▶ chemical compounds (e.g. a new cleaning product)
- ▶ mixtures of compounds (e.g. an improved perfume).

Recent litigation has even concerned patents for chemical processes and vaccines.

NATURE OF PROTECTION

Patent protection does not arise automatically and the filing of an application for a patent, followed by its being granted, is necessary in order to obtain protection.

The protection permits the inventor to stop third parties from using, producing, importing or selling the invention without permission. It gives the inventor exclusive rights in the country where the patent is granted, provided renewal fees are paid on a yearly basis.

Patents are *territorial* rights – therefore if granted in the UK, the holder will have rights only in the UK. If you want to secure protection in other countries, you can apply in that country or, in Europe, through the European Patent Convention or the Patent Co-operation Treaty.

Is it important to always remember that you must not publicly reveal your invention before you apply for a patent – doing so could risk the chances of your being granted one.

A granted patent becomes property, and therefore you can buy, sell, license or even use it as mortgage security, just as you would with any other property. Equally, you may be able to buy or license patents belonging to others.

You cannot patent your invention if it falls into the category of:

▶ a scientific or mathematical discovery, theory or method
▶ a literary, dramatic, musical or artistic work
▶ a way of performing a mental act, playing a game or doing business
▶ the presentation of information, or some computer programs
▶ an animal or plant variety
▶ a method of medical treatment or diagnosis, *and*
▶ anything immoral or contrary to public policy.

TERM

Patents in the UK have a duration of 20 years from their filing date, subject to payment of renewal fees and not being invalidated.

INFRINGEMENT

There are two kinds of acts that infringe registered patents under the Patents Act 1977. These are direct and indirect infringement.

Where a *product* is concerned, **direct infringement** occurs when a person, without the owner's consent, makes, disposes of, offers to dispose of, uses or imports the invention. Infringement does not require the person involved to have any knowledge of the infringement.

In relation to a *process*, direct infringement occurs if a person, without the owner's consent, uses the process or offers it for use in the UK, when it would have been clear to a reasonable person that its use would amount to an infringement.

In comparison, when a person supplies or offers to supply any of the means relating to an essential element of an invention for putting the invention into effect, this will amount to **indirect infringement**.

DEFENCES TO INFRINGEMENT

Under section 60 of the Patents Act 1977, the following statutory defences are available:

▶ where an act is done privately and for purposes which are not commercial, it does not amount to an infringement
▶ where an act is done for experimental purposes which relate to the subject matter of the invention there can be no infringement

- the extemporaneous preparation in a pharmacy of a medicine for an individual in accordance with a prescription given by a doctor does not amount to an infringement
- in relation to ships – an act which consists of the use, exclusively for the needs of a relevant ship, of a product or process in the body of such a ship or its machinery, tackle or apparatus or other accessories in a case where the ship has temporarily or accidentally entered UK waters, does not amount to an infringement. Similar protection also extends to aircraft, hovercrafts and vehicles.

REMEDIES FOR PATENT INFRINGEMENT

An aggrieved patentee may claim the following remedies in court-based dispute resolution:

- an injunction to prevent further infringements that led to the dispute in the first instance
- damages to compensate for loss suffered as a consequence of the infringement or an account of profits made by the infringer as a result of the infringement
- an order that the infringing articles that are the subject of the dispute be destroyed or delivered up, *and*
- a declaration that the patent was valid and infringed.

Trade marks

WHAT IS PROTECTED?

A trade mark is any sign that can be represented graphically and which can distinguish your goods and services from those of other traders.

A sign may consist of:

- words (e.g. NIKON for cameras)
- slogans (e.g. 'Keep the flag flying' for British Airways)
- designs (e.g. the apple for Apple Inc.)
- letters (e.g. WWF for World Wildlife Fund)
- numerals (e.g. Chanel No. 5)
- Internet domain names (e.g. moneysupermarket.com)
- sounds (e.g. MGM's lion's roar)

► colours (e.g. Tiffany & Co.'s registration of the blue on its distinctive jewellery boxes), *or*
► a combination of the above.

NATURE OF PROTECTION

Registering your trade mark affords you the right to use the mark on the goods and services in the classes for which they are registered. This allows you to take legal action against anyone who uses your mark or a similar mark on the same or similar goods and services to those that are set out in the registration.

For registration to be obtained, your trade mark must be:

► distinctive for your goods and services, *and*
► not the same as, or similar to, any earlier marks on the register for the same, or similar, goods or services.

What is 'distinctive'?

It is important to remember that your application for registration can be rejected if the words, logos, pictures or other signs are unlikely to be seen as a trade mark by the public. For example, marks which describe goods or services or any characteristics of them; terms that have become customary in your line of trade; terms that are not distinctive (e.g. slogans); or a combination of these will *not* be possible to register.

However, invented words or even dictionary words that are not in any way associated with your goods or services are accepted as being distinctive.

Earlier marks

Your application can be objected by the owner of an earlier mark if the mark is considered to be so similar that it causes confusion. In order to find out if there are existing similar registrations, you should contact the Intellectual Property Office (IPO; www.ipo.gov.uk). If you proceed with your application to register, the IPO will contact all owners of earlier registrations so that, when the application is published in the *Trade Mark Journal*, they can oppose it if they wish to.

Two identical marks can be registered if there are sufficient differences between the goods or services. It is important as a business to be aware of other trade marks being applied for in the UK. If you consider a mark to be too similar to your own, you can choose to oppose it.

You do not need to register a trade mark. As an unregistered trade mark you will acquire rights under common law by using the TM symbol. However, it is much easier to enforce rights if you register you mark and use the ® symbol to indicate that it is registered.

Like patents, a trade mark can be sold, leased or licensed for use by another trader.

TERM

In order to remain in force, a trade mark must be renewed every ten years from the date of filing. Provided that this is done, it can be maintained indefinitely.

INFRINGEMENT

Trade mark infringement occurs where a registered trade mark is used without the owner's consent in any of the following circumstances:

▶ The sign used is identical to the registered trade mark and is used in relation to goods or services which are identical to those for which the trade mark is registered (section 10(1), Trade Marks Act 1994 (TMA)).
▶ The sign used by the infringer is identical to the registered trade mark and is used in relation to the goods or services which are similar to those for which the trade mark is registered, or the sign is similar to the registered trade mark and is used in relation to goods or services which are identical or similar to those for which the trade mark is registered, and in each case there exists a likelihood of confusion on the part of the public, which includes a likelihood of association (section 10(2), TMA).
▶ The sign used by the infringer is identical or similar to the registered trade mark, the trade mark has a reputation in the UK, and the use of the sign, being without due cause, takes unfair advantage of, or is detrimental to, the distinctive character or the repute of the trade mark (section 10(3), TMA).

Table 3.1 gives a summary of what constitutes trade mark infringement under the Trade Marks Act 1994:

Table 3.1   Circumstances which constitute infringement under section 10, Trade Marks Act 1994

Section	Sign	Goods/ Services	Other qualification
10(1)	Identical	Identical	
10(2)	Identical	Similar	Likelihood of confusion
10(2)	Similar	Identical	Likelihood of confusion
10(3)	Identical or Similar	Any	Registered mark has a reputation + use is without cause + takes unfair advantage/ is detrimental to distinctive character/ repute of mark

DEFENCES TO INFRINGEMENT

Section 11 of the TMA sets out various defences to trade mark infringement:

▶ *'Own name' Defence* (s. 11(2)(a), TMA). A registered trade mark is not infringed where a company, business or person uses their name and address as a trade mark. The name has to be one by which they are called or usually known.
▶ *The use of indications concerning the kind, quality, geographical origin and other characteristics of goods or services* (s. 11(2) (b), TMA). Use of these characteristics will not constitute an infringement of a registered trade mark.
▶ *The use of a trade mark where it is necessary to indicate the intended purpose of a product or services (in particular, accessories or spare parts)* (s. 11(2)(c), TMA). There will be no infringement of a registered trade mark where it is necessary to use it to indicate the intended purpose of goods or services.

In order to rely on the above defences, the use must be in accordance with honest practices in industrial or commercial matters.

The remedies available to a successful claimant in a trade mark infringement action are similar to patent infringement and include:

▶ injunctions
▶ damages or an account of profits
▶ orders for erasure, removal or obliteration of offending signs from infringing goods, materials or articles, *and*
▶ orders for delivery-up and destruction of infringing goods, materials or articles.

Copyright

Copyright seeks to protect the *form of expression* of ideas and not the ideas themselves. The primary purpose is to reward authors for the creation of original works – that is, works where the author has expended independent effort to create the work.

Copyright law is intended to prevent copying. However, it does not provide a monopoly right; similar or identical work may exist provided it has not been copied.

WHAT IS PROTECTED?

Section 1(1) of the Copyright, Designs and Patents Act 1988 (CDPA) states copyright exists in various types of works and protects the following:

▶ original works (s. 1(1)(a), CDPA), which include literary, dramatic, musical or artistic works
▶ sound recordings, films or broadcasts (s. 1(1)(b), CDPA), *and*
▶ typographical layout of published editions (s. 1(1)(c), CDPA).

The Act grants the owner a series of exclusive rights, which prevent any other using their work without their permission.

Original works
A literary, dramatic, musical or artistic work must be original in order to qualify for copyright protection. The author must have created the work through his/her own skill, judgement and individual effort and must not have copied from other works.

Copyright protection for literary, dramatic, musical or artistic works is only afforded where the requirement of fixation is satisfied – that is, that the copyright is recorded, in writing or otherwise.

LITERARY WORKS

This is defined as any work written, spoken or sung, other than a dramatic or musical work (section 3(1), CDPA). The purpose of this right is to give protection to the expression of ideas and information that can be expressed in words of some form, provided the work created is original.

However, attempts to protect a single word or a small number of words have failed because these lack the necessary requirement of originality.

The most obvious type of literary work are things such as books, poems and instructions of some sort, but the definition extends to things such as compilations, computer programs, databases, ordinary business letters and examination papers. This list is not exhaustive.

DRAMATIC WORKS

A dance or mime which can be recorded in some way and capable of being performed constitutes a dramatic work (section 3(1), CDPA) – for example, the script of a play, a screenplay for a television programme, or a choreographed dance routine, with or without words or music, which was capable of performance.

MUSICAL WORKS

Musical works are defined as works consisting of music, exclusive of any words or action intended to be sung, spoken or performed with the music.

ARTISTIC WORKS

An artistic work is defined as:

▶ a graphic work, photograph, sculpture or collage, irrespective of artistic quality, *or*
▶ a work of architecture being a building or a model for a building, *or*
▶ a work of artistic craftsmanship.

Artistic works are not required to have any artistic quality and will be protected regardless. However, following case law, artistic craftsmanship requires some aesthetic appeal.

Sound recordings, films or broadcasts
SOUND RECORDINGS
These are defined as a recording of:

- ► sounds, from which the sounds may be reproduced, *or*
- ► all or part of a literary, dramatic or musical work, from which sounds reproducing that work or part may be produced.

The first category is intended to cover recordings of sounds which are not based on underlying literary, dramatic or musical works, such as a recording of a bird singing, while the second category would include recordings of existing copyright works.

Sound recordings are protected regardless of the medium on which the recording is made or the method by which the sounds are reproduced or produced. However, copyright does not subsist in a sound recording which is a copy taken from a previous sound recording.

FILMS
A film is defined as a recording on any medium from which a moving image may be produced, whatever the means of doing so. It is the material that is recorded, not the subject matter of the film, which is protected by copyright.

There is no requirement of originality.

BROADCASTS
A broadcast is an electronic transmission of visual images, sounds or other information, which is transmitted:

- ► for simultaneous reception by members of the public and is 'capable of being lawfully received by them' (first limb), *and*
- ► at a time determined solely by the person making the transmission for presentation to members of the public (second limb).

However, Internet transmissions are excluded, unless they are:

- ► transmissions taking place simultaneously on the Internet and by other means

- ▶ concurrent transmissions of a live event, *or*
- ▶ transmissions of recorded moving images or sounds which form part of a scheduled programme service.

Typographical arrangements

This copyright affords protection to the layout of literary, dramatic and musical works. However, it is important to remember it is not necessary for any of these works to already be subject to any copyright in themselves to be afforded typography copyright.

In the UK, no formalities are needed for a work to receive copyright protection; protection automatically applies to all works recorded in any form provided that they meet certain requirements.

TERM

You can use the © symbol followed by your name and the date to indicate when it was created and by whom.

It is possible to license, sell or transfer by assignment your copyright to someone else. However, if you decide to use someone else's copyright in your business, you should always remember to get permission from the individual or organization that owns the copyright first.

Table 3.2 provides a summary of the **terms of copyright protection** – that is, the periods of time for which copyright is protected:

Table 3.2   Summary of terms of protection under Copyright, Designs and Patents Act 1988

Copyright	Term of protection
Literary, dramatic, musical and artistic works	Lasts for the creator's lifetime plus 70 years
Films	70 years after the death of the last of the directors, score composer, dialogue or screenplay authors
Broadcasts	50 years from the first broadcast
Sound recordings	50 years
Typographical arrangements	25 years from creation

INFRINGEMENT

There are two different types of infringing acts:

1. **primary infringement** – which does not require knowledge or intention on the part of the infringing party, *and*
2. **secondary infringement** – where specific knowledge is required at the time of the offence.

Primary infringement

A person must not, without the consent or licence of the copyright owner, do any of the following acts:

▶ copy a copyright work
▶ issue copies of the copyright work to the public
▶ rent or lend the work to the public
▶ perform, show or play a copyright work in public
▶ communicate the work to the public
▶ make an adaptation of a copyright work or do any of the acts listed above in relation to an adaptation.

It is also an infringement for you to instruct another to do any of the above.

Secondary infringement

Table 3.3 gives a summary of secondary infringement:

Table 3.3   Secondary copyright infringement

Infringing acts	Knowledge or belief with which act must be carried out
In relation to an article which is an infringing **copy**: • importing into the UK, other than for private and domestic use • in the course of a business, possessing, exhibiting in public, or distributing • selling, letting for hire, or offering or exposing it for sale or hire • distributing it to such an extent that will prejudicially affect the copyright owner.	Knowledge or reason to believe that the article is an infringing copy

Table 3.3 Secondary copyright infringement (*continued*)

Infringing acts	Knowledge or belief with which act must be carried out
In relation to **articles specifically designed or adapted for making copies** of a copyright work: • making such article • importing into the UK • possessing it in the course of a business • selling, letting for hire, or offering or exposing it for sale or hire.	Knowledge or reason to believe that the article is to be used to make infringing copies
Transmitting a copyright work via a telecommunications system (e.g. transmission by fax or email)	Knowledge or reason to believe that infringing copies of the work will be made by means of the reception of the transmission in the UK or elsewhere
Giving permission for use of a place of public entertainment for a performance which has infringed copyright in a literary, dramatic or musical work	The person who gave permission is liable unless, when he/she gave permission, he/she believed, on reasonable grounds, that the performance would not infringe copyright
Supplying apparatus for playing sound recordings, showing films or receiving visual images or sounds conveyed by electronic means, or a substantial part of such apparatus, which has been used to perform, play or show a copyright work in public so as to infringe copyright	Knowledge or reason to believe that the apparatus was likely to be used to infringe copyright; *or* Where the normal use of the apparatus would involve a public performance, playing or showing, lack of belief on reasonable grounds that it would not be used to infringe copyright

(*continued*)

Table 3.3 Secondary copyright infringement (continued)

Infringing acts	Knowledge or belief with which act must be carried out
Giving permission, as occupier of premises, for such apparatus, or a substantial part of such apparatus, which has been used to perform, play or show a copyright work in public so as to infringe copyright, to be brought on premises	Knowledge or reason to believe that the apparatus was likely to be used to infringe copyright
Supplying a copy of a sound recording or film which has been used, with such apparatus, to perform, play or show a copyright work in public so as to infringe copyright	Knowledge or reason to believe that the copy of the sound recording or film, or a copy made from it, would be used to infringe copyright

DEFENCES

In order to bring a successful claim of copyright infringement, you must be able to show:

▶ copyright subsists in work in the UK
▶ that you are the owner of the copyright in the work
▶ the defendant copied your work, *and*
▶ the defendant copied the whole or a substantial part of the work, so as to amount to an infringement of the copyright of the claimant.

There a varied degrees of defences to counter a claim of copyright infringement.

First, a defendant could argue that one or more of the above criteria have not been met. It has also been argued in the courts that there is a common law defence – namely, that the infringing act was done to satisfy public interest (e.g. that it was necessary in order to accommodate the right to freedom of expression).

REMEDIES

The remedies available to a successful claimant in a copyright infringement action include:

▶ award of damages or an account of profits
▶ injunction
▶ orders for delivery-up and/or destruction of infringing works
▶ additional damages if it is proved that the defendant flagrantly infringed copyright and/or obtained a benefit from the infringement.

Overview

Table 3.4 gives an overview of the various protections available in the United Kingdom:

Table 3.4 Summary of intellectual property protection under UK law

	Patents	Trade marks	Copyright
Term	Up to 20 years (subject to annual renewal)	Rights can last forever (renewals every 10 years)	Life plus 70 years; broadcast and sound recording copyright lasts 50 years and typographical arrangement for 25 years
Protection	Throughout the UK	Throughout the UK	Throughout the UK and much of the world
Protects against	Idea being manufactured, used or sold	Use of trade mark without your permission	Work being copied or reproduced in communication or performance
What is protected?	Inventions	Brand identity, including logos and signs	Literary works, music, broadcast, art and film

TEST YOURSELF

1 Patent protection obtained in the UK automatically protects the right worldwide. True or false?

2 Patent protection in the UK lasts for...
   (a) five years
   (b) 20 years
   (c) 25 years
   (d) life plus 50 years

3 You must apply to obtain copyright protection. True or false?

4 Is a company's database of business contacts protected by copyright?
   (a) yes – in the UK
   (b) only if you tell everyone it is
   (c) no
   (d) really not sure

5 Your business has a logo and a distinct brand identity which you want to protect. Do you...
   (a) obtain patent protection
   (b) obtain copyright protection
   (c) obtain trade mark protection
   (d) do none of the above because you can't?

4

....

Employment

In this chapter you will learn about:
- *what, as an employer, you should be aware of in the employment relationship from recruitment through to termination of employment*
- *dealing with problems during the employment relationship*
- *restrictive covenants.*

Introduction

Achieving a good relationship with your employees is crucial, particularly in a small business where employees can be the life blood of the business. Much of the employment relationship is governed by legislation, and is also subject to frequent change due to European influences and our own government.

Employment law is often described as a 'minefield' with tripwires crossing the employer's path at every turn. This may be a somewhat pessimistic assessment. However, it is true that employment law is complicated and therefore it is important to be well informed and to act reasonably wherever possible. This chapter will give you an indication of what to be aware of from the start of the employment relationship to the end, and how to avoid problems if they arise.

Recruitment

Getting the right staff is very important. A business will want to make sure that it is recruiting staff who are capable of doing the job, and who will work well with existing employees. However, employers will need to make sure that they do not discriminate in the recruitment process.

ADVERTISEMENTS

Advertisements must not (even unintentionally) discriminate against any applicants. Wherever possible, make adverts factual, and make sure you only ask for things that are essential for the job – for example, don't ask for 'young and...'. Also, avoid words that could be seen as discriminatory – for example, words like 'energetic' could suggest only young people should apply.

Be careful about insisting on qualifications, academic or otherwise. Unless they are essential, you should make it clear that equivalent experience or qualification is acceptable so as to avoid any claim of age or racial discrimination. If you say you need a particular type of person, experience, skill or qualification, you need to be able to justify it. Remember, excluded or unsuccessful candidates can bring discrimination claims.

Before any recruitment process you need to be clear what the job will involve and what attributes are essential. You may want to create a job specification (what it involves) and a person specification (which skills are essential and which are desirable).

You can use application forms to ask candidates particular questions. For example, if the role involves complaints handling, you could ask them about dealing with a customer complaint.

Alternatively, you can ask for CVs. It is usual to request a covering letter with a CV, to allow candidates to tell you why they want/are suited to the job.

You should not ask about a candidate's health, except to ascertain whether they need reasonable adjustments for the recruitment process. You have a duty to provide reasonable adjustments to candidates with disabilities and should tactfully explore what, if anything, they need. After you have made an offer of employment to an employee with a disability, you should explore what, if any, reasonable adjustments are required for them to do the job and, with their consent, you may need to get medical advice or occupational health reports.

SELECTION PROCEDURES

Selection procedures vary widely depending on the type of role that needs to be filled. Common procedures include: tests (verbal, numerical, data interpretation, psychometric, practical and/or case studies), group exercises and presentations. There are companies which specialize in helping with selection procedures.

It is up to you which procedure(s) you use, but they must be appropriate and fair. You should be testing only those skills that the candidates will need for the job and you should treat all candidates in the same way (with an exception for those requiring reasonable adjustments).

INTERVIEWS

Interviews are the most common way of assessing the suitability of candidates. It is good practice for at least two people to conduct any interview. This is usually someone with human resources (HR) experience and the person who will be managing the role.

A successful candidate will then usually be asked back for a second interview, with someone more senior who has the authority to decide whether to hire them.

You may want to show candidates the workplace and introduce them to their potential colleagues. Sometimes this is done in an informal setting (e.g. over lunch). Remember, any informal conversations are part of the interview process and can give rise to claims.

Ideally, decide on a list of relevant questions to ask all the candidates. While you may want to explore different aspects of each candidate's background, ultimately, you need to know the same things about them to work out who is best for the job.

Interview questions

The most common types of interview questions are:
1 experience based (e.g. 'How many people did you manage?')
2 competency based (e.g. 'Can you tell me about a time you worked in a team?')
3 understanding based (e.g. 'What do you know about our organization/the job?')
4 character and motivation based (e.g. 'What are your weaknesses?', 'What do you want in a job?').

All questions should be directly relevant to the job. You need to be careful about asking questions that could be seen as discriminatory (e.g. about family arrangements). If you decide to ask such questions, make sure you ask them to all the candidates (e.g. don't ask only women candidates about childcare). Think about *how* you are asking questions (e.g. if the work involves fixed hours, ask candidates if they anticipate any difficulties with this, rather than asking if they have family commitments).

Example

This role involves working on a Sunday...

Do ask

Are you available to work on a Sunday? We operate a shift pattern...

Don't ask

You don't go to church do you?

Do ask

Are you able to work in the evenings?

Don't ask

We don't want any women with kids – you aren't planning on having kids, are you?

Take good notes and keep records of all interviews and your decision-making process. You should consider each candidate carefully against the key requirements of the role and make your decision based on their respective merits. You may have to justify your decision to a court, so the more evidence you have that an appropriate and fair process was followed the better. When retaining notes of interviews you must comply with the Data Protection Act 1998. Please see Chapter 9 for an overview of data protection issues.

REFERENCES

When you have decided whom to appoint, you should get references. It is usual to ask for two references, often one from their previous employer and one personal reference. Many employers provide only standard references, including factual information such as start date and job title.

You may want to speak with the referees as well as getting a written reference as you may get a fuller picture with a conversation.

You should ask the candidates when you can approach their referees. Usually, they will ask you not to approach their current employer until after you have offered them the job. It is important to make any job offer dependent on receiving satisfactory references and, if necessary, medical/occupational health reports.

GIVING A REFERENCE

References are an important part of employing people (and being employed) and therefore are an important part of operating a business. There are a lot of fears about giving a reference; however, with the use of sensible caution and following a few rules, the reference process can be managed well and no one needs to suffer unreasonably.

The fears stem from a series of legal cases over the last 15 to 20 years, and in some situations an aggrieved employee may sue the employer if the reference given is wrong or false and that falsity leads to damage to the employee's career. The case of *Spring v Guardian Assurance*, a House of Lords case of 1994, won by Bevans, established that an employer owes an employee a duty of care not to write a negligent reference. The employer in that case described Mr Spring as a 'man of little or no integrity who cannot be regarded as honest'. Unsurprisingly, he was unable to work again in financial services. The reference was carelessly false and Mr Spring recovered substantial damages.

The problem
On the one hand, there is a duty on an employer to give a reference that does not mislead the *recipient* – usually another employer; on the other hand, there are some clear guidelines set out in recent case law that boil down to the proposition that an employer also owes a duty to the *subject* of a reference not to write or say something that is not:

- ▶ true
- ▶ accurate, *and*
- ▶ fair

…though it does not have to be full and comprehensive.

The *recipient* of a reference can also sue if the reference is false and damages are suffered. A significant case was one where one educational establishment gave a good or reasonable reference to another education college and failed to mention that the *subject*, a swimming and PE coach, had convictions for paedophiliac behaviour. The subsequent scandal at the new school caused substantial losses.

By adhering to the rule that there must be no misleading and sticking to the three bullet points above, you should be safe from claims from either side.

Do you *have* to give a reference?

The answer is normally 'no' but beware of the following situations:

▶ Where you are in an industry or sector where a reference must be provided such as financial services or in areas involving children.

▶ Where you want to avoid an argument by an employee that you have victimized them by not providing a reference when others have been given one or because the employee has taken you to an employment tribunal.

Where you want to have a policy of not giving anything other than a basic factual reference (e.g. 'She worked for us for three years as a secretary'), then it is a good idea to document this. You will then have some protection, against the claim above that it was unfair not to give a fuller reference. Remember, though, that if you favour someone you like or may want to have back working for you and give a fuller reference, then your policy is breached and this may result in claims by other less-favoured departing staff.

Should you give a reference?

This is a different question. Why would you want to give a fuller reference? The answer may be that with a number of departing people it is good business policy – and good ethics – to help them in their further career. Many sectors are small and like 'villages'. Harsh treatment can bounce back and a no-reference policy does create problems for leavers, particularly if they have been long-serving and loyal and have no other people to get job references from. This is ultimately a judgement call by the managers of any business.

How to go about writing a reference

Giving a reference amounts to processing data under the Data Protection Act 1998 (DPA). Normally, this would require the consent of the subject. However, under Schedule 2(6) of the Act, disclosure is allowed in respect of non-sensitive information which a third party has a 'legitimate interest' in receiving. There might be doubt and so where possible, or at least where sensible and possible, the employee should sign a consent to the reference being given. However, that may, in turn, lead to them asking to see the reference!

Examples of sensitive information are information about ill-health and also about misconduct which amounts to the commission of a criminal offence. These are tricky areas and consent should be sought or advice taken from a lawyer.

Finally, but importantly, the DPA does not give the subject the right to see the reference. This is an exemption for the person or entity writing or giving the reference. The recipient of the reference may not be so exempt and in time the Act may be used by the subject to extract a copy.

The need to be able to show that care has been taken

This is because the law considers the giving of a reference to be a situation akin to dismissal and the care taken needs to be equivalent to that taken by a fair employer trying to avoid an unfair dismissal case.

Care is needed not only in writing the reference but also in preparing it from properly kept documents and other records. Often these records will be personnel files. In different fields, there will also be, for example, records of such things as policy/ business persistency or other key performance indicators. In health situations, complaints files will contain important information upon which later references may have to be written. It is vital that all relevant staff know what documents need to be maintained and that regular checks are made to ensure they are being kept to a sufficient standard. Litigation is now much more common than it was, say, 25 years ago and more people are aware that a bad reference can be the 'kiss of death' to a career, making it more likely they will claim if something goes wrong.

Businesses need these records for other purposes and the DPA applies in many situations, and so in well-run organizations there should not be a problem. Beware of, however, a situation where a number of branch offices all keep a part of the story. A reference does not have to be complete but a partial story is much more likely to be unfair.

The matters typically covered in a reference will be:

- length of employment
- position held
- honesty
- competence
- timekeeping
- sickness record
- reasons for leaving
- within reason, answers to specific queries from the new employer.

Confidentiality – can it be relied upon?
The short answer is no. Both under the DPA (in the hands of the recipient) and in litigation (disclosure rules), it is likely that a disgruntled employee will get to see the reference. No longer is it safe to say to the recipient 'this is sent in confidence and must not be disclosed to X'. Verbal references are perhaps at first glance safer, but do you trust the person at the other end of the telephone? Best policy is to be frank and truthful and fair, and to be prepared for the employee to see the reference.

Some classic references

- 'You will be lucky to get this man to work for you.'
- 'It takes him an hour to get to work... after he has got there.'
- 'This should be enough to crucify him.' (in the Spring case cited above)

Employment status

During the recruitment process you will need to ask yourself whether your staff will be employees or workers or self-employed. Although the question is simple, the answer is likely to be complicated and uncertain. The courts are regularly asked to find the answer because employees have more employment rights than workers and the self-employed.

There is no user-friendly definition of 'employee' or 'worker' or 'self-employed' and as a result the courts have developed a number of different tests to find the answer; in essence, the tests look at the relationship between the parties.

If the individual is under the **control** of the 'employer', then the individual is likely to be an employee. Control includes:

▶ setting the individual's hours and place of work
▶ telling the individual what tasks to complete, and how to complete those tasks
▶ providing the individual with facilities and equipment to undertake their tasks.

It is also important to look at whether there is **mutuality of obligation** between the individual and the employer (i.e. is the employer obliged to provide work, and is the individual obliged to accept work?). How the parties treat the working relationship is another relevant factor. If the individual is paid through PAYE, is paid for holidays and sickness absence and/or has their expenses reimbursed, then these are all factors that point towards an employment relationship.

If the individual can meet the requirements described above, then they are likely to be an employee. If the individual only meets some of the requirements above, then they are likely to be a worker. It is important to remember that it doesn't matter what 'label' is applied to the working relationship: calling someone a 'worker' doesn't mean that they are not an employee.

The self-employed

You may have staff who work on a self-employed basis. If an individual is genuinely self-employed (i.e. they are registered as self-employed with HMRC), they use their own equipment and resources, and are free to work for other businesses, then they are unlikely to meet the legal definition of employee or worker.

WHAT RIGHTS DO EMPLOYEES AND WORKERS HAVE?

Does it matter whether your staff are employees or workers? Yes, because employees have more rights than workers. As the question of status is not straightforward, you should always take advice about the rights of your workforce. Table 4.1 gives guidance on the different rights that can apply to employees and workers:

Table 4.1 Summary of the different rights that can apply to employees and workers

Right	Employee	Worker
Section 1 statement	Yes	No
To claim unfair dismissal	Yes (after 1 year)	No
Redundancy payment	Yes (after 2 years)	No
Protection from discrimination	Yes	Yes
Minimum wage	Yes	Yes
Statutory sick pay	Yes	No
Paid annual leave	Yes	Yes
Maternity/Paternity pay	Yes	No
Statutory notice	Yes	No

A small business has a bookkeeper come in a couple of times a week. She completes her time sheet at the end of the week, and at the end of the month is paid through PAYE. She is free to choose when she works. She works at the business's premises and uses their IT equipment. Although she has fixed responsibilities, she is free to choose what tasks to complete and when.

Question: Is she an employee, a worker or self-employed?

Answer: She probably isn't an employee as there is a lack of control over her and her work, there appears to be no obligation on her to accept the work, and she is not treated as an employee by the business. However, she could be a worker, as she uses the business's equipment and is paid through PAYE. She could therefore be entitled to holiday pay.

AGENCY WORKERS

A business will sometimes have agency workers who are provided by an employment agency. Agency workers are commonly used to fill short-term vacancies (e.g. for holiday cover), but if the agency worker works for the business for some time they are likely to become incorporated into the business, and it is likely that the business has quite a lot of control over them. However, they are unlikely to have any employment relationship with the business. This is because they are normally employees or workers of the agency, and the agency has responsibility for them, rather than the business.

Under the Agency Workers Regulations 2010, which came into force on 1 October 2011, agency workers do have a right after 12 weeks with a business to the same basic working and employment conditions as employees of the business. These include conditions relating to pay, duration of working time and annual leave, but do not include sick pay or pension payments. They also have a right in relation to accessing the business's facilities and amenities, and a right to be informed of any vacancies within the business.

If the business fails to offer the agency worker comparable terms, or treats them differently or dismisses them because they have complained about their terms and conditions, then the agency worker could bring a claim against the business including a claim for unfair dismissal, even if they have been employed for less than a year.

Employment documents

There are likely to be a number of documents dealing with the employment relationship. All employees should have a written statement or contract of employment. The business may also have a staff handbook and other separate policy documents, such as a disciplinary and grievance policy.

GETTING IT IN WRITING

The law usually treats verbal and written contracts as valid. However, with verbal contracts it is sometimes difficult to prove what was agreed. It is therefore good practice to get written evidence for any important agreements, signed by the relevant people. If you don't have clear agreement in writing, then it may ultimately be up to a court to decide what you agreed.

EMPLOYMENT CONTRACTS

There is an employment contract between an employer and employee; just because there is no written contract, this does not mean that there is no contract. Therefore, a contract of employment can be verbal or in writing. There is a legal requirement to provide employees (or give them easy access to), within two months of them starting employment, a written statement of the key terms of employment. This is called a **section 1 statement**.

The section 1 statement: key terms

Key terms include:

▶ employee and employer names
▶ the date employment begins and, if it isn't permanent, how long for / when it will end

- when the employee's continuous employment began (taking into account any employment with a previous employer which counts towards that period)
- remuneration or how it is to be calculated
- when the employee is to be paid (e.g. monthly)
- conditions relating to hours of work
- holiday entitlement including public holidays
- conditions relating to holiday and sick pay and pension schemes
- notice employee is entitled to give and receive.
- job title or description of duties
- the place of work or, where the employee works in various places, acknowledgement of this and the address of the employer
- details of collective agreements that affect the terms and conditions of employment
- where the employee is required to work outside the UK for a period of more than one month, the period to be worked, the currency remuneration to be paid in, any additional remuneration and benefits to be provided, and conditions relating to return to the UK
- details of disciplinary and grievance procedures, including job title/name of those who will be involved in the process.

If key terms are not applicable, the section 1 statement should say so. Some of the information (e.g. disciplinary procedures) can be in different documents. The section 1 statement then says where the information can be found (e.g. in the staff handbook).

Most employers prefer to provide a more detailed **employment contract,** which should also incorporate the key terms. What should go in an employment contract depends on the type of job and the business's needs. The employment contract should reflect what is required. A director's contract will be different to one for a junior employee and may include restrictive covenants (discussed later in this chapter). You should get expert advice to ensure you provide employment contracts.

The law can imply (write in) terms into contracts, even if you have not included them. These can be terms set out in law (e.g. the minimum wage, statutory holiday and sickness entitlement), or terms that reflect the reality of the working relationship (e.g. something that is custom and practice in your industry or workplace).

When preparing the contract of employment, you will need to think about what type of contract you need. For example, the work may be available only for a fixed period of time, or the work may come to an end at a particular point, i.e. when a project is finished. You may also want to consider whether the contract is temporary, reflects a casual working arrangement, or is seasonal. Different rules apply to different types of contract, and therefore you should take advice when preparing contractual documents.

A sample basic contract of employment can be found in Annex 1 near the end of this book.

Other types of employment documentation

A key consideration for employment documentation is whether it is contractual. You need to consider carefully what should be a contractual term and what is a policy. The most important things (e.g. wages) are usually considered contractual terms. It is more serious to break a contractual term and you can be sued for it. If you do not want things to be contractual, you need to make it clear in the documentation that they do not form part of the employment contract. However, it may ultimately be up to a court to decide whether or not a document or part of it is contractual, but the court will take into account how it is labelled.

You should keep all employment documentation up to date.

STAFF HANDBOOKS

Employers usually have a staff handbook or separate documents containing policies and procedures. Exactly what policies you need will depend on your business and you will want to take specific advice on this, but you should always reserve the right to vary your policies and procedures and make this clear in the documents.

Some examples of common policies

- ▶ health and safety
- ▶ rewards and benefits
- ▶ training
- ▶ expenses
- ▶ sick pay
- ▶ parental rights
- ▶ bad weather
- ▶ home working
- ▶ capability, disciplinary and grievance
- ▶ appraisal, promotion and recruitment
- ▶ equal opportunity
- ▶ gifts and referrals

LETTERS

Sometimes you will want to write to an employee (e.g. giving them a pay rise). Such letters may become part of the contract of employment and should be carefully worded.

CONFIDENTIALITY AGREEMENTS

If an employee deals with confidential information, you may want to get them to sign a separate agreement reinforcing the confidentiality and detailing how they are to deal with such information both during and after their employment.

Varying terms and conditions of employment

You should make sure you have a variation clause in the employment contract which allows you to vary its terms. But even then you cannot unilaterally change an employee's terms and conditions. Employees must be told within one month of any changes coming into effect.

Best practice is to consult with your employees and get their agreement in writing to any changes. Changing working conditions is a very risky business and often leads to tribunal claims. You should always seek appropriate legal advice before changing terms and conditions.

Family rights – as at May 2011

Employees are entitled to a number of family rights. These include:

► maternity leave and pay
► paternity leave
► parental leave
► a right to request flexible working.

MATERNITY LEAVE

All employees, irrespective of their length of service, are entitled to maternity leave.

At least 15 weeks before the baby is due, the employee must notify her employer that she is pregnant, when the baby is due, and when she intends to start her maternity leave. Maternity leave cannot start earlier than 11 weeks before the baby is due. An employee can change the date her maternity leave starts, although she must give at least 28 days' notice.

The employee does not have to give written notification, although a business can ask for the details to be put into writing. Once an employee tells a business when she plans to start her maternity leave, the business must within 28 days tell her when the maternity leave will end – the starting assumption is that the employee will take her full 52 weeks entitlement. If the employee wishes to change her return date, she must give at least eight weeks' notice.

It is good practice to have a dialogue on maternity leave with an employee at an early stage, as this will help the business plan to cover her absence.

The employee also has a right to paid time-off for antenatal care, and the business may be required to carry out a health and safety assessment once the employee notifies them that she is pregnant.

You should remember that you cannot treat an employee differently because she is pregnant, or because of maternity leave. If you do treat the employee differently, then this could be discrimination (see below).

MATERNITY PAY

In order to qualify for statutory maternity pay, an employee must have been employed for at least 26 weeks for the period up to 14 weeks before the baby is due. She must also give at least 28 days' notice of when she expects her maternity pay to start. Statutory maternity pay cannot start earlier than 11 weeks before the baby is due.

If the employee meets the above requirements, she is then entitled to:

▶ 6 weeks at 90 per cent of average weekly earnings; *then*
▶ 33 weeks of statutory maternity pay, or 90 per cent of average weekly earnings, whichever is lower.

An excellent online tool for calculating maternity entitlement is available on the Directgov website (www.direct.gov.uk/maternity.dsb).

PATERNITY LEAVE

In order to qualify for paternity pay, an employee must be:

▶ employed for at least 26 weeks for the period up to 14 weeks before the baby is due
▶ the father of the child, or married to or in partnership, or civil partnership, with the mother, *and*
▶ expecting to have responsibility for the upbringing of the child.

No later than 15 weeks before the baby is due, the father must tell his employer when the baby is due, how long his paternity leave will be (either one week or two consecutive weeks) and when he intends the paternity leave to start. Paternity leave can be taken up to 56 days after the baby is due (or born, if earlier). An employee's statutory paternity pay is equivalent to statutory maternity pay.

In certain circumstances where the mother returns to work before the end of her full maternity leave entitlement, additional paternity leave of up to 26 weeks is available.

PARENTAL LEAVE

This right extends to employees with not less than one year's service who have, or expect to have, responsibility for a child.

Parental leave entitles the employee to up to 13 weeks' unpaid leave for each individual child, and to be taken by the time the child reaches five. The employee may take only up to four weeks in any year, and must give the employer 21 days' notice that they intend to take parental leave. The employer can refuse the request for parental leave if the operation of the business would be unduly disrupted, but the employer must allow the employee to take the leave at another time within the next six months.

FLEXIBLE WORKING

In general terms, a parent of a child aged 16 or under, or of a disabled child aged 18 or under, and who has been employed for at least 26 weeks, can make a request for flexible working. A flexible working request can include changing the hours of work, the time of work and the place of work.

A business must consider a request for flexible working in accordance with a strict procedure. This includes meeting with the employee to discuss the request, confirming the decision in writing, and, if the request is rejected, offering the employee an appeal. The business can refuse the request if particular grounds apply, which include:

▶ a burden of additional costs
▶ a detrimental effect on customer demand, quality or performance
▶ inability to reorganize work among existing staff or recruit additional staff.

Dealing with problems

Where people work together, problems in the workplace can happen; these can range from staff having disagreements with each other or personality clashes, to serious disputes about treatment or changes to employment conditions. How you deal with these problems is important; remember to try to be reasonable and wherever possible keep good written records.

AVOIDING PROBLEMS

▶ Always be careful how you communicate with and treat your employees. Encourage employees to be open and come to you with problems so you can take a proactive approach.
▶ It is often helpful to understand what is behind any problems. For example, it may be that the employee has problems at home, or is struggling with his/her workload. Identifying the problem quickly can help identify a solution before the problem gets out of hand. For example, offering the employee some flexibility in terms of his/her hours, or providing him/her with additional training or support at an early stage can help diffuse problems quickly.

- ▶ If the employee is being bullied or feels he/she is treated differently, this can give rise to tribunal claims if not handled appropriately. If you address problems quickly and tactfully, you may be able to deal with them informally before they become serious. Good communication, including regular formal appraisals, regular informal feedback and appropriate training (e.g. equal opportunities), all help to achieve this.
- ▶ Be tactful and professional in all communications with employees (e.g. do not be rude to them or suggest they are not up to the job). If the relationship breaks down, you may find yourself defending a constructive unfair dismissal claim.
- ▶ Keep good written notes of meetings with employees and any appropriate thought processes you go through regarding employees. Such notes can be vital evidence to show that you have behaved in a fair and reasonable way. You should keep up-to-date personnel records, including details of any disciplinary measures.

The ACAS Code of Practice on disciplinary and grievance procedures

If the problem cannot be resolved at an early stage, then the employee may raise a grievance, or you may want to start disciplinary proceedings. All disciplinary (including capability) and grievance procedures and policies must conform to the **Code of Practice of the Advisory, Conciliation and Arbitration Service** (ACAS). Tribunals have the power to increase compensation by 25 per cent for failure to follow the Code (or reduce it by 25 per cent if the employee doesn't follow it).

You should also follow your own disciplinary, grievance and/or capability policy if you have one. If it is contractual, you may face a breach of contract claim if you don't.

Capability (performance) issues are covered by the Code, as well as misconduct. Where there are capability issues, employers are expected to give employees appropriate time and support (e.g. training/extra supervision/equipment) to improve.

It is beyond the scope of this book to cover the Code or these procedures in detail. You can obtain a copy of the Code and detailed guidance on it at www.acas.org.uk and you should always seek appropriate advice to deal with any employment issues.

Any procedure and any action you take in relation to employees should be reasonable and fair in all the circumstances. You should give employees enough time to consider the situation and any evidence, and an appropriate chance to put their point of view.

There are five basic steps in a formal disciplinary or grievance procedure:

1 The employee or the employer raises the issues in writing.
2 Investigation by the employer.
3 A meeting is held.
4 Decision is made, employee informed in writing of the decision and right to appeal.
5 Appeal.

However, you will need to adapt these steps to the situation – for example, where the employee provides new evidence that requires further investigation. The key is that the procedure is fair and reasonable.

You must not prejudge the outcome. It must be clear to the employee that no decision has been reached until after all appropriate evidence has been properly considered, and the employee has had a chance to put their point of view.

Procedures should be completed in reasonable time. What is reasonable will depend on the situation, but it is sensible to try and deal with issues quickly. However, you need to make sure that any investigation is thorough and that employees have sufficient time to prepare for meetings, including gathering supporting evidence.

Depending on the findings of a grievance or capability procedure, you may then need to conduct a disciplinary procedure. In some circumstances, you may need to report wrongdoing to outside agencies (e.g. a government or professional organization).

WRITTEN COMMUNICATIONS

Written communications should be clear and should contain all the necessary information. For example, letters inviting employees to disciplinary meetings should include details of the issues, potential disciplinary consequences, the right to be accompanied and who will be dealing with the procedure as well as details of the meeting. It is important that you inform the employee in writing of their rights (e.g. the right to be accompanied).

PEOPLE INVOLVED

All those involved should be independent; this means that they should not have had anything to do with the issues or any reason to be biased. For example, if an employee has complained about a particular manager, this manager should not handle the disciplinary or grievance process. Those making decisions should be senior to the employee and, wherever possible, any appeal should be heard by someone senior to the person who made the initial decision. If you have a small business, then you will need to think carefully about who will handle the first stage of the process, and who will be available to handle any appeal.

Ideally, any investigation should be carried out by a person not involved in the meetings. If you are a small organization, you may want to consider appointing independent people to conduct some or all of the procedure. Many HR consultancies offer this service.

RIGHT TO BE ACCOMPANIED

Employees are legally entitled to bring a colleague or a trade union representative to disciplinary or grievance meetings. The role of the accompanier is detailed in the Code.

In certain serious cases (e.g. where their ability to continue in the profession may be at stake), employees may be entitled to legal representation.

Sometimes an employee will ask to have a friend or family member accompany them. While you do not have to permit this, you may choose to do so.

MEETINGS

Meetings should be held in appropriate surroundings. This will include ensuring any meeting is held in a private room where other colleagues cannot overhear. In some circumstances, particularly when the employee is not at work, you may want to consider holding the meeting outside the workplace.

The decision maker should always be supported by a colleague so the organization has at least two representatives at any meeting. The colleague should be responsible for taking clear and detailed notes, and the employee should be given a copy and asked to agree it. Any changes the employee wants can be recorded separately if you do not agree to them. Some people choose to record meetings and use the transcript.

It is important to give the employee time to make all their points. You can ask questions and you should not make a decision until you have seen/heard all the relevant evidence and had appropriate time to consider.

INVESTIGATIONS AND EVIDENCE

Investigations should be thorough. Employees should see any evidence and be able to comment on it if they wish to do so. Sometimes evidence may be confidential (e.g. witness statements from colleagues who are concerned about reprisals). You can provide anonymous copies or a full summary of the evidence. In very unusual circumstances, you can withhold evidence (e.g. if producing it puts someone in danger). However, there is a presumption that employees have a right to see and comment on the evidence. If they do not get this chance, a procedure may be unfair.

Any investigation should be tactfully handled. Remember, employees may be coming back to work and it is important you do not damage their reputation or make it difficult for them to do their job, or you may be facing a claim.

DISCIPLINARY MEASURES

It is vital that disciplinary measures are appropriate and reasonable; for example, it is unlikely to be reasonable to dismiss an employee for being slightly late on one isolated occasion.

The usual types of disciplinary measures are: informal warnings, formal verbal warnings, formal written warnings (usually first, second and third/final for repeated or escalating offences) and, finally, dismissal.

Warnings should have clear expiry dates. Most warnings last between six months and one year, but how long a warning should last will depend on what is reasonable in the situation.

In some very unusual circumstances, expired warnings may be taken into account, but it is risky to do this and you should always seek appropriate legal advice in these circumstances.

SUSPENSION

Sometimes it is necessary to suspend an employee while an investigation or other procedure takes place. You should not suspend an employee for longer than is reasonably necessary. It is important that you never give the impression that the outcome is prejudged, so any suspension will usually be on full pay and it must be clear it is not a punishment.

GROSS MISCONDUCT

If you have incontrovertible evidence that an employee has done something bad enough to break the employment relationship (e.g. a significant theft), you may be able to dismiss them immediately for gross misconduct. You should, however, always take appropriate legal advice before doing this because circumstances where you can dismiss without following the Code and a proper procedure are very rare and it is best practice to follow the Code.

The Equality Act 2010

The Equality Act 2010 is the main piece of legislation dealing with **discrimination**. There are also Codes of Practice that offer guidance on the Act, which courts can take into account. The Codes are available on the Equality and Human Rights Commission website (www.equalityhumanrights.com).

Discrimination law is complex and often changes. This chapter is not legal advice or a legal guide. Specific and personal legal advice should be taken on any individual matter.

PROTECTED CHARACTERISTICS

The Equality Act makes it unlawful to discriminate against someone on particular grounds; these are known as **'protected characteristics'**. There are nine protected characteristics: sex, age, race, religion and belief (which includes lack of belief), sexual orientation, pregnancy and maternity, marriage and civil partnership, disability and gender reassignment. You need to remember that discrimination can apply to these protected characteristics in many ways – for example, it can be unlawful to discriminate against a man and age discrimination applies to both young and old.

Religion and belief is also wide-ranging, and 'belief' has been held to include a philosophical belief in the dangers of climate change, spiritualism and anti-hunt views.

TYPES OF DISCRIMINATION

Direct discrimination

Direct discrimination is where a person is treated less favourably than another because of a protected characteristic. This could include refusing to employ someone because of their race, or preventing women from applying for promotion.

Indirect discrimination

Indirect discrimination is usually more subtle than direct discrimination and is where a practice, provision or criterion is applied across the board but disadvantages people with a particular protected characteristic. This could include having a shift pattern that indirectly affects women who are more likely to have childcare commitments, or requiring all staff to work on a Sunday, which could indirectly affect staff with religious commitments. The key is that all staff are treated the same, but staff with a protected characteristic are disadvantaged.

There may be a defence to a claim of indirect discrimination if you can show that the provision, criterion or practice is a proportionate means of achieving a legitimate aim. For example, applying a length-of-service provision in redundancy selection criteria could be indirectly discriminatory because it puts younger employees at a disadvantage. However, where the provision was intended to reward loyalty and provide a stable workforce, and the provision was only a part of the redundancy selection criteria, then this could be a proportionate means of achieving a legitimate aim, and therefore a defence to a claim of age discrimination.

Victimization

Victimization is a word that is sometimes used in the workplace in connection with bullying. However, under the discrimination legislation it has a very specific and limited application. A person can be victimized if they can show that they have been subjected to detriment because they have done 'a protected act'. A protected act includes alleging discrimination, bringing a discrimination claim, or supporting someone making a complaint about discrimination. If someone does a protected act, and then is treated differently or suffers detrimental treatment (e.g. not being awarded a bonus), then this could be victimization.

Harassment

Harassment is unwanted behaviour that has the purpose or effect of violating a person's dignity or causing a degrading, hostile, humiliating, intimidating or offensive environment. This could include bullying someone because of their sexuality or engaging in 'banter' which could offend women.

In some circumstances, employers may also have a duty to protect their staff from harassment by third parties. For example, if a receptionist is harassed by a particular customer, the employer knows about this and fails to take reasonably practicable steps to prevent the harassment, a court could decide that the employer is guilty of harassment.

Discrimination by association or perception

Discrimination by association or perception is a relatively new concept.

'Association' is where someone doesn't have a protected characteristic themselves, but is associated with someone who is. For example, an employee who cares for a disabled child would be associated with someone with a protected characteristic. If the employee is treated less favourably because they care for a disabled child, this could be discrimination on the grounds of disability by association.

'Perception' is where an employee is treated less favourably because someone thinks they have a characteristic that is protected, even if they don't actually have that characteristic. For example, if an employee was bullied for being homosexual, even though he wasn't homosexual, then this could amount to discrimination on the grounds of sexuality by perception.

Reasonable adjustments

An employer has a duty to make reasonable adjustments for disabled employees if they are at a substantial disadvantage compared to people who are not disabled. They may be disadvantaged by a provision, criterion or practice, a physical feature or lack of special equipment. Examples of reasonable adjustments include providing specialist equipment or allowing flexible working hours. Whether or not an adjustment is 'reasonable' depends on several different factors. Some examples are cost, effect on other employees and the organization.

Employers can sometimes get help from the government with the cost of reasonable adjustments.

Instruction to discriminate

It is unlawful to tell someone to discriminate (e.g. to tell a recruitment agent to send you only young candidates).

Occupational requirements

Sometimes a job requires a particular protected characteristic (e.g. a priest who needs to have a particular religion, or an actor who must be of a particular race). This is called an **occupational requirement**. If you can objectively show that there is an occupational requirement for a role, you can employ only those who fulfil that requirement.

Objective justification on grounds of age

If you can show it is objectively justified, you can make decisions based on someone's age. For example, if you need to be very physically fit to be, say, a firefighter and there is good evidence that people over a certain age cannot be fit enough, then you could decide not to recruit an older person to the role. It is very unusual to be able to objectively justify age discrimination and very risky to make decisions based on age.

POSITIVE ACTION AND THE BENEFITS OF DIVERSITY

Having a diverse workforce has lots of benefits. Different types of people can bring new views and ideas to your business, and help you expand into new sectors.

Positive action is a legal way of encouraging unrepresented/ disadvantaged groups to apply to and work with your organization.

Positive action is voluntary, and shouldn't be confused with **positive discrimination,** which is unlawful. You can find out more about positive action in the Act and the Code of Practice on Employment on the website of the Equality and Human Rights Commission.

PENALTIES

Legal penalties include financial compensation, a declaration that your organization was discriminatory and/or a recommendation as to what you should do to put things right.

Discrimination claims can also seriously damage an organization's reputation and may count against you if you bid for certain types of work (e.g. public sector work). Public sector organizations have to consider the public sector equality duty and organizations that work with the public sector may have to consider this, too.

PROTECTING YOUR ORGANIZATION

Employers can be responsible for the actions of their employees, as well as any agents they work with, such as consultants or recruitment agencies. In certain circumstances, they can also be responsible if employees are harassed by third parties (e.g. customers). Individuals can be sued for discriminatory behaviour (e.g. the employer and the employee can both be sued).

It is helpful to:

▶ have equal opportunities policies and training on equal opportunities
▶ never make assumptions about people with protected characteristics
▶ make sure you treat people fairly and as individuals
▶ make it clear that your organization will not tolerate discrimination and deal with allegations of discrimination appropriately
▶ ensure that your employees know how to get help if they feel they have been discriminated against
▶ have appropriate and transparent selection processes for recruitment and promotion, and appoint the best candidate to the role.

Transfer of undertakings – TUPE regulations

The TUPE regulations are designed to protect the workforce when there is a transfer. This protection includes preserving the contract of employment and the terms of employment (such as pay) when a transfer takes place, and giving an employee a right to claim unfair dismissal if they are dismissed because of a transfer.

The regulations apply to two distinct situations:

1 *Where a business or part of a business is sold or otherwise acquired by a new owner.* The legal test is whether there has been a transfer of an economic entity which retains its identity. Indicators that there has been a TUPE transfer include whether what is being done by the new business is essentially the same thing as was done by the old business, whether staff have transferred and whether assets have been transferred.
2 *Where there is a service provision change.* This occurs where a service is outsourced to an external contractor, where an outsourced service is brought back in-house or where the identity of the external contractor providing an outsourced service changes.

Bloggs and Co. provides cleaning services to ABC Council under a service contract. Following a retendering process Bloggs loses the contract to Toddle Waddle Ltd. This is a service provision change and the employees of Bloggs who were assigned to the ABC Council contract will transfer their employment to Toddle Waddle. If, a few years later, ABC Council decides it wants to bring the service back in-house, then this will again be a service provision change and the staff will transfer to the employment of ABC Council.

Where there has been a transfer or a service provision change, then all employees in the part of the business transferred move to the new business on exactly the same terms and conditions and their continuity of service is preserved. Any dismissal of staff for a reason connected to the transfer will be unfair unless there is an economic, technical or organizational reason entailing a change in the workforce (e.g. a genuine redundancy situation).

If your business is bidding for any outsourced contracts, then you must consider whether TUPE will apply and whether you will then inherit new staff. It is important that you undertake full due diligence in advance so that you know what the staff liabilities may be.

If your business intends to acquire another business or a part of another business, TUPE could apply and so again you must undertake detailed due diligence on what staff liabilities may be transferred.

Termination of employment

Bringing an employment relationship to an end is very much the last resort. For most owners or managers of a small business it is not a pleasant thing to do, and therefore sometimes it is put off when actually a decision should have been taken much earlier to end someone's employment.

Before commencing any dismissal procedure you should always take detailed advice, as the dismissal of an employee for a reason other than one allowed by law, without following the correct procedure, or without giving adequate notice, is likely to lead to a claim for unfair and/or wrongful dismissal. The damages for a successful claim can be significant and regardless of whether a claim succeeds, the costs of defending it, both in terms of legal fees and management time, may be substantial.

It is always worth remembering that ordinarily an employee must have at least one year's continuous service in order to bring an unfair dismissal claim – there are exceptions such as for whistle-blowing and health-and-safety-related dismissals but these are outside the scope of this book. Therefore, if you have an employee with less than one year's service, provided you give them the proper notice, and provided you are not discriminating against them, then you can normally bring their employment to an end quickly and safely – in particular, there is no legal need to follow a detailed and fair procedure as the employee will not be able to claim unfair dismissal and so will not be able to challenge the procedure used. However, it is best practice to follow a fair dismissal process in all cases as it helps to reduce resentment and bad feeling in the workplace.

HOW CAN EMPLOYEES WITH MORE THAN A YEAR'S SERVICE BE DISMISSED LAWFULLY?

1 *There must be a fair reason for the dismissal.* Fair reasons are limited to:
   - ▶ conduct
   - ▶ capability or qualifications
   - ▶ redundancy
   - ▶ where continuing to employ the employee would be illegal (e.g. as a result of their immigration status), *and*
   - ▶ where it is for 'some other substantial reason' (SOSR).
   A dismissal for any other reason would be unfair.
2 *The employer must follow a fair procedure.* Even if there is a potentially fair reason for dismissing an employee, an employer must still follow an appropriate fair procedure before deciding whether to dismiss. The particular procedure that must be followed for each potentially fair reason differs and is outside

the scope of this book but, generally speaking, the employee must be told of the possibility of dismissal and allowed to put forward any reasons why they should not be dismissed. They should also be allowed an appeal. The ACAS Code of Practice should also be followed if applicable – see above.

3 *The employer must act 'reasonably'.* What is reasonable will vary depending on the reason for dismissal. For example, where an employee is being dismissed because they are not capable of doing the job, an employer will usually have to give the employee a chance to improve and provide reasonable support or training to the employee to make the necessary improvements. All the circumstances, including the size and resources of the employer, will be relevant when determining whether an employer acted reasonably.

4 *The employee should be given the correct period of notice.* Except in cases of gross misconduct, employees have a right to receive a period of notice if they are dismissed. The period of notice is normally specified in the contract of employment and it must not be shorter than the statutory minimum amount of notice (one week for each complete year of service up to a maximum of 12 weeks). An employee may be required to work during their notice period, although an employer may have the contractual right to make a payment in lieu of notice instead. Whether the employer has such a right will depend on the terms in the contract of employment. If the employer fails to give proper notice or to make payment in lieu before dismissing an employee, this is likely to amount to a wrongful dismissal, for which the employee can claim loss of earnings and benefits to which they would have been entitled during their notice period.

Some practical steps to reduce risk

▶ Try to resolve problems as soon as they arise.
▶ Think carefully about any emails (or other written correspondence) sent to employees. For example, never send any aggressive emails.
▶ Keep records of any emails, letters, conversations or meetings (formal or informal) with employees relating to their conduct or performance.

> ► Do not sideline, bully or shun an employee to get him/her to leave. This could give an employee a constructive unfair dismissal claim.
>
> ► Fully investigate any claims made by or against an employee and allow him/her to put their side of the story at a meeting before making any decision.
>
> ► Do not assume that someone can be dismissed simply because his/her fixed-term contract has come to an end. You will still need a fair reason and a fair procedure.
>
> ► If an employee has raised a grievance or claim in the past, ensure that any further allegations against that employee are dealt with fairly to avoid the risk of a victimization claim.

REDUNDANCY

It may be necessary for an employer to make an employee redundant. A redundancy occurs when an employer:

► ceases to carry on the business for the purposes of which the employee was employed to do

► ceases to carry on the business in the place the employee worked

► ceases or diminishes work of a particular kind, *or*

► ceases or diminishes work of a particular kind in the place the employee worked.

Redundancy is a fair reason for dismissal, but the employer must follow a fair process, which will include consulting with the employee and identifying any suitable alternative work. There are different rules for consultation depending on how many employees are to be dismissed for redundancy. ACAS have a useful guide on handling redundancy which can be found on its website: (www.acas.org.uk).

If any employee is dismissed for redundancy, they are entitled to a statutory redundancy payment, calculated with reference to their age, length of service and weekly wage (subject to a statutory cap).

Restrictive covenants

A **restrictive covenant,** or post-termination restriction, is an agreement between employer and employee that seeks to restrict the employee's activities after they have left employment. They typically seek to prevent the employee working for a competitor, working with clients of the business and poaching employees of the business. They are also usually for a fixed period of time after the end of employment, and are sometimes limited to a particular geographical area.

Restrictive covenants are common in contracts for senior employees, or for employees who work in sales, and are a useful tool for businesses seeking to protect themselves.

If a business wants to protect its interests in the future, it will need to ensure that restrictive covenants are contained within a written contract of employment. It should make sure it has a copy of that contract of employment signed by the employee. A business can seek to introduce restrictive covenants after the employee has started working for the business, although there is no guarantee that the employee will accept them.

If there are restrictive covenants written into the contract, the business must also be able to show that the purpose of the restriction is to protect its legitimate business interests (e.g. the business's **trade connections**). To be enforceable, restrictions must not be more than is **reasonably** necessary to protect the employer's legitimate business interests.

Some definitions

Trade connections – This generally means the business's customers, clients, suppliers, and senior or key employees. It does not necessarily include former or potential future customers and clients, or more junior employees, and careful drafting is needed if such items are to be included within the scope of a restriction.

Reasonable – Much will depend on the facts of the particular case, but reasonableness is likely to include the seniority of the employee, the real need to protect the business, the duration of the restriction, and the geographical area to which the restriction applies. If the business can show that the restrictive covenants are reasonable, then in principle they are binding on the employee.

An employee worked for the business for three years and was a sales manager. He was responsible for selling a product to more than a hundred different clients in East Anglia. He knew the procurement officer for each client, knew their budget, their product needs, and, of course, knew how much the product was sold for. He resigns and joins a competitor. The business is concerned that the employee could be contacting all their clients and undercutting the business on price. The employee had restrictive covenants in his contract of employment preventing him from working with a competitor in the region for six months, and from contacting the business's clients for six months after he left employment.

In the above example, it looks like the employee is in breach of his restrictive covenants, and therefore the business can bring a claim against the employee. They can apply to the court for an injunction forcing the employee to comply with his restrictive covenants, and they can also bring court proceedings against the employee for breach of contract and seek to recover damages from him for the loss the business has suffered as a result of his actions.

In the above example, if the employee did not have any restrictive covenants in his contract of employment, then it would be very difficult for the business to prevent his future actions or bring court proceedings against him.

A business can also seek to protect itself by placing an outgoing employee on **garden leave** during their notice period. This means that, although the employee is still paid, they are not required to attend the workplace. As a result, they will not have any contact with key clients and will not know of any changes to the business's prices or contacts. A business should place an employee on garden leave only if there is a specific garden leave clause in the contract of employment.

The employment tribunal

If there is a dispute between an employer and employee, the case will usually be dealt with by an employment tribunal, rather than a court.

If an employee wants to make a complaint to the employment tribunal, in most circumstances they must do so within three months less a day from the act complained of.

If an employee makes a claim, they will complete a form known as an **ET1**. The employment tribunal will send the employer a copy of the ET1, and the employer must respond within 28 days using the form **ET3**.

After the ET1 and ET3 have been received, the tribunal may arrange a **Case Management Discussion** (CMD). The CMD is an administrative hearing designed to prepare the case for final hearing. The **employment judge** will normally want to know what the dispute is about, and he/she will also make orders or directions dealing with the disclosure of documents, the exchange of witness statements, and the date and length of the hearing.

At the final hearing, there will normally be a panel of three people hearing the case. These are: an employment judge, who is a qualified lawyer with experience in employment law, and two 'members'. There will be one member with an 'employee' background, often a union official, and an 'employer' member, usually someone with a business or HR background.

Tribunal hearings are designed to be less formal than court hearings – for example, all the parties are seated, even when speaking to the employment judge or when giving evidence. There is no requirement for either party to be legally represented, although often parties are represented by a solicitor, barrister or employment adviser.

It is unusual in the employment tribunal for the loser to pay the winner's legal costs. Normally both parties bear their own costs, win or lose, unless one party has acted unreasonably, vexatiously or abusively.

If an employee presents a claim to the employment tribunal, you may want to consider settling that claim. ACAS are involved in the tribunal process as third-party conciliators. They are independent of the tribunal and the parties, and will assist the parties in resolving their dispute.

Further information on employment tribunals can be found here: http://www.justice.gov.uk/guidance/courts-and-tribunals/tribunals/employment/index.htm.

TEST YOURSELF

1 Which of the following can you safely ask applicants about in a job application form?

(a) date of birth

(b) whether they have childcare commitments

(c) their sexuality

(d) their qualifications

2 You employ a part-time ad hoc worker in your accounts department. They are entitled to...

(a) sick pay

(b) holiday pay

(c) maternity pay

(d) help themselves from the till

3 You must give an employee a written statement of main terms and conditions of employment...

(a) within two months of commencing employment

(b) within four months of commencing employment

(c) when you get round to it

(d) when there is a problem and you then back-date it

4 You are a manager and you think a member of your team is pregnant. She must notify you...

(a) as soon as she is aware

(b) at least 15 weeks before the baby is due

(c) after her 12-week scan

(d) when she starts craving gherkin ice cream

5 You are commencing disciplinary action against a member of your team and you arrange a disciplinary hearing with the employee concerned. They have a right to...

(a) be accompanied by a family member

(b) be accompanied by a solicitor

(c) be accompanied by a colleague or trade union representative

(d) be obstructive to your investigation and do what the hell they like

6 Which of the following protected characteristics are covered by the Equality Act 2010?

(a) marital status

(b) fundamental belief in climate change

(c) disability

(d) belief in the tooth fairy

7 Your business is successfully awarded a contract by a local authority to provide the cleaning services for its schools. Your fiercest rival currently provides the service. Will you...

(a) be able to sack all the current employees carrying out the work without fear of claims

(b) have to take on the current staff under TUPE as it is a service provision change

(c) inform and consult with the current staff and then cherry-pick the good ones leaving the rest behind with your competitor while you gloat

(d) sit back and let your competitor clean up the problem!

8 A member of your team has been with your company for eight months. You want to dismiss him because he has not performed as well as you had hoped having seen him come sixth on *The Apprentice*. Do you...

(a) call him to a meeting, tell him it has not worked out and service him with his contractual notice period in writing

(b) go through a full performance management process identifying what improvements need to be made, giving him six months to improve and providing him with reasonable support, training and assistance to make such improvements and, if no such improvements are made, commence a formal process of written warning, final written warning and then dismissal

(c) declare his role redundant

(d) call him in for an old-fashioned rollicking and then afterwards let him carry on regardless

5

···

Contracts: an overview

In this chapter you will learn about:
- *contracts and contract law in general terms*
- *the key components of a contract – agreement, form, intention and consideration*
- *the key factors to consider when looking at or entering into contracts.*

Definition

Perhaps surprisingly the law does not provide a formal definition of what a contract is. The definition we shall be using for the purpose of this chapter is as follows and is the very root of what a contract is:

> A contract is an agreement which the parties intend to be legally binding.

The cardinal principle this definition embodies is: **freedom of contract.** We will see that it also encompasses a number of substantive elements and these will be described below.

Parties to a contract

Before looking at the fundamental components of contracts, it is worth spending some time considering what we mean by 'the parties'. A contract must have at least two parties. It is not possible to have a sole party to a contract; it is not possible to sue oneself.

The vast majority of contracts that small businesses come across or enter into are between two parties and are described as **'bilateral'** or **'bipartite contracts'**. There are numerous contracts between more than two parties. However, to illustrate the key principles of contract law, we will confine ourselves to bilateral contracts. The general principles will apply to all types of contracts irrespective of the numbers of the parties.

'The party' is the entity which has the legal personality and power to enable it to enter into a contract. This capacity is specifically described as **contractual capacity**. For a legal person to be able to enter into a contract, that person must have full contractual capacity. There are exceptions that relate to specific and certain categories of individuals, authorities and companies. The contractual capacity of an individual is restricted if he/she is a minor or if he/she has a mental disorder or is intoxicated. A minor is an individual under the age of 18 at the time that the contract is entered into. What is relevant is the individual's actual age, not his/her apparent age or the age he/she claims to be or his/her maturity. Whether an agreement with a minor is enforceable depends on the nature of the agreement.

Registered companies

Each registered company has a written constitution. This generally consists of two documents: the **memorandum of association** and the **articles of association**. The memorandum of association lists the activities which that company is authorized to engage in (known as the company's 'object'). A company only has the capacity to enter into contracts in furtherance of its objects. The rule used to be that, if it entered into any other contract, that contract was *ultra vires* (meaning beyond the powers of the company) and void. This meant that a third party had to be careful when contracting with a company to ensure that the company's objects were broad enough to give it the power to enter into that contract.

The Companies Act 2006 fundamentally altered the position. It provides that the validity of an act done by a company cannot be called into question by reason of anything in the company's memorandum of association. This does not mean that a company now has full contractual capacity: in principle, its contractual capacity is still limited by reference to the objects set out in its memorandum. But it does mean that a third party dealing with a registered company in good faith no longer has to concern himself/herself with the contents of that company's memorandum. Effectively, therefore, a third party can assume that a company has full contractual capacity as long as he/she is not actually aware of any limitation imposed by its memorandum.

Agreement

We will now look at the key components of a contract.

We have stated a contract is an **agreement**. Lawyers often use the word 'agreement' to refer to the formal document signed by the parties, and many people wrongly believe that this is what a contract is. In our definition, however, the word 'agreement' refers to when the contracting parties are in the same mind about something. To say there is an agreement necessarily implies that the contracting parties have communicated with each other. The law has a distinctive and useful way of analysing these communications in order to identify the precise point at which agreement is reached. These are the principles of **offer** and **acceptance**.

OFFER

Let us look firstly at the offer. The party that makes the offer is described as the **offeror** and the party that receives the offer as the **offeree**. An offer is a definite and unequivocal expression of willingness to contract on specific and specified terms with the intention to become binding as soon as it is accepted by the party to whom the offer is addressed.

The offer may be:

▶ actual (either written or oral) or implied from conduct
▶ made to a particular person or group of persons, or to the world at large.

An offer must be:

▶ definite and unequivocal
▶ made with a clear intention to be bound by it (not a negotiating point) and it must be communicated

REVOCATION

An offer may be terminated by revocation, rejection or lapse. For revocation to occur, it must be made by the offeror before acceptance and may be communicated by a third party.

REJECTION

Rejection is the express turning down of the offer by the offeree by making a counter-offer, and it is important to note in this context that a request for further information or clarification is not a counter-offer.

LAPSE

This occurs when, before acceptance, a specific time limit for acceptance expires or one or more conditions attached to the offer fail, or if the offeree dies. It must be noted that there is a very important distinction between an offer and **'an invitation to treat'**. An invitation to treat is a statement expressing a willingness to receive offers. It is not an offer in itself. Rather, this is an invitation for others to make offers. Examples of this are shop displays, advertisements, catalogues and prospectuses.

Statements of intention and statements of price are also not offers to sell. In the former, the intention to sell is not the same as an offer to sell. In the latter, the response to a request to indicate price is also not an offer to sell.

ACCEPTANCE

Acceptance is the final and unconditional assent to the terms of an offer. On this basis it must correspond exactly with the offer. It must be unconditional and unequivocal. The principle whereby valid acceptance must correspond exactly to the offer is sometimes referred to as the **mirror image rule**. Since acceptance must be communicated, it follows that silence can never constitute acceptance. So the sentence 'Unless I hear from you I shall assume you accept' does not carry the weight normally attributed to it. The communication of acceptance may be oral, written or by conduct. If the offeror stipulates a mode of acceptance, the offeree must comply with this form. It is different if the offeror suggests a mode of acceptance.

Tenders

As an invitation to tender is usually an invitation to treat, the submission of a tender is usually considered an offer. The acceptance of a tender, however, does not always result in a binding contract. Generally, one-off tenders are fully binding once the tender is accepted. Again, where a tender is submitted for supplying a specific quantity of goods over a specific period of time, acceptance results in a binding contract. Where a tender is submitted for an indefinite subject matter or amount, then the tender does not result in a binding contract until that aspect is defined.

Auctions

In auctions, the lot itself, or the putting up of a lot, is considered an invitation to treat. Each bid represents an offer to buy the lot at the price offered and lapses on the making of subsequent bids. Acceptance occurs when the auctioneer 'knocks down' the lot to the highest bidder. Until the lot is knocked down, any bidder may retract their bid. If an auctioneer has advertised the existence of a reserve, acceptance of a lower bid will not be valid.

Not every agreement is a contract

It will be clear that not every agreement is a contract. Two people may agree that Chelsea will win the Premier League this season, but this agreement is not a contract because it does not involve either party undertaking to do anything. The law of contract is concerned with agreements where the parties undertake to do something (or, sometimes, *not* to do something).

Let us look at the simplest possible commercial transaction to identify the agreement and see what the parties undertake to do. Suppose that I were to go into a newsagent's to purchase a newspaper with the marked price of 50 pence. I say '*The Times*, please.' The newsagent puts *The Times* on the counter and says 'Fifty pence, please.' I pay him the money and leave with the paper. The only piece of paper involved is the newspaper itself, but the legal analysis of this transaction is that a contract has been both entered into and performed. The newsagent entered into an agreement with me. The terms of which were that he undertook to supply me with *The Times* and I undertook to pay him 50 pence. In other words, he assumed the obligation to supply a newspaper and I had a corresponding right to one, while I assumed the obligation to pay him 50 pence and he had a corresponding right to that sum. We both performed our obligations. With more substantial commercial contracts, the parties may wish to make a written record of the agreement or draw up a formal written agreement or there are standard terms.

An agreement in writing has the great practical advantage of leaving less room for doubt about what the parties agreed and undertook to do. It is for this reason that substantial commercial transactions almost always have at their heart a written agreement which has been fully negotiated and reviewed by each party's lawyers.

FORM

While common law imposes no specific form in line with freedom of contract, there are a number of examples of legislation requiring particular kinds of agreement to be in a particular form, and these are the exception to the general principle that the parties are free to enter into an agreement in any form they choose. Even contract law textbooks do not always list these statutory exceptions as most concern agreements of a specialized nature. There are three general forms that apply by statute to specific contracts. These are:

1 a deed
2 an agreement in writing, *and*
3 an agreement evidenced in writing.

Over time, formal and substantive requirements for executing deeds have been relaxed. However, deeds must follow a specific form and be executed in a specified manner. The types of contract requiring deeds include conveyance of land, an assignment of a lease over three years and the transfer of a ship.

Contracts which *must* be in writing include bills of exchange, maritime insurance contracts, consumer credit agreements, company share transfers, assignments of debts and contracts for future sale of land.

The most important categories that must be supported by written evidence are guarantees.

Guarantees

Under section 4 of the Statute of Frauds 1677, a guarantee cannot be enforced against the person who gave it unless he/she has signed the guarantee or some other document which records its terms.

A guarantee is a contract under which one person undertakes to do something if another person fails to do it. The obligations of a guarantor are therefore described as '**secondary obligations**'.

In practice, guarantees are almost always in writing. You will notice, however, that section 4 does not actually require contracts of guarantee to be in writing, but only that the guarantor must have signed either the guarantee or some other document which records the terms of the guarantee if it is to be enforceable against him/her. So, an oral guarantee is enforceable if, for example, the guarantor confirms the arrangements in a signed letter.

Intention

MEANING

An agreement is only a contract if, at the time the parties entered into it, they intended that agreement to be legally binding. If they did, then either party can go to court to enforce the other party's obligations to him/her under the agreement, and the court will enforce those obligations unless there is some other factor which makes the contract invalid. If, on the other hand, the parties did not intend their agreement to be legally binding, then that agreement is not a contract and neither party can go to court to enforce it. The phrase '**contractual intention**' is used to describe the parties' intention to be bound to the agreement.

INFERRING INTENTION

In respect of the intention of the parties, a fundamental issue is that, while lawyers think in terms of contractual intention, other people generally do not. People enter into all kinds of agreements without stopping to think whether or not they intend those agreements to be legally binding. Unless the parties have made their intention clear, it is necessary to infer what their intention was. If the parties had been asked the question at the time the agreement was entered into, would they have said that the agreement would be enforceable through the courts?

The courts have dealt with this and have sought to distinguish agreements that should be legally enforceable and those which should not, in an effort to avoid being troubled by disputes concerning agreements which were not intended to be legally binding. These fall into a number of categories: social and domestic agreements, commercial agreements and advertisements.

Agreements between husbands and wives and parents and children are presumed not to create legal relations. In respect of husbands and wives, this is the case unless the agreement itself states that it does.

In respect of parties who are not related sharing a house, the courts will consider the circumstances of the agreement.

Whereas in respect of social and domestic arrangements there is a presumption that there is no intention to create legal relations, in commercial agreements it is presumed that there is an intention to create legal relations and this presumption can be rebutted only by express provisions in the contract.

Generally speaking, domestic arrangements are not intended to be legally enforceable, but commercial arrangements are. So my son cannot successfully sue me (despite his threats to do so!) if I fail to pay the pocket money I agreed to give him, nor can I successfully sue someone who agrees to come to dinner but fails to turn up (although I would often like to!). On the other hand, there is no doubt that the agreement with the newsagent for the sale of the newspaper is legally enforceable.

There are times when the parties' intentions can be extremely difficult to infer.

EXPRESS INTENTION

It is unnecessary to infer the parties' intentions if they have expressly stated them. If a particular agreement is expressed to be **legally binding** (or is expressed not to be legally binding), that express intention is conclusive. There are, of course, other ways of putting it without using the phrase 'legally binding'. The words 'binding', 'enforceable' or 'contract' all serve to indicate contractual intention.

THE BURDEN OF PROOF

If a party to an agreement claims that it was intended to be legally binding, the burden of proving it is on him/her to satisfy the court of that fact. With a substantial commercial agreement involving significant sums of money and valuable goods or services, it will be very difficult to convince a court that there was no contractual intention unless this was expressly stated. It is inherently unlikely for example that the Royal Navy would agree to buy an aircraft carrier on the basis that it could not sue the seller if the carrier proved defective, and it is equally unlikely that the seller would agree to sell it on the basis that he/she could not sue for the purchase price. In practice, very few claims for breach of a commercial agreement are defended on the grounds that there was no contractual intention, and those that are nearly all relate to interim agreements.

CONSIDERATION

Consideration is one of the essential elements of the binding contract (unless it is made by deed). When an offer, acceptance, intention to create legal relations and consideration are present, an agreement becomes contractually binding. English law does not and will not enforce a gratuitous promise. If your 19-year-old son promised to mow the lawn but then does not, the courts will not deal with it (even though it might meet with a judge's sympathy!). The consideration may take the form of payment or some other service. Definition of consideration arises from case law.

There are three fundamental rules in respect of consideration that have become established in case law. These are:

1 *That consideration must move from the promisor.* What this means is that a person to whom a promise was made can enforce that promise only if they themselves made the consideration. This is not the case if the consideration is given by a third party.
2 *Consideration must not be historic and consideration must be sufficient but need not be adequate.* This effectively means that, as long as the consideration has some value, the courts will not concern themselves with its adequacy – i.e. whether it represents a good or a bad deal.
3 *Consideration must be real, tangible and valuable* – i.e. it must have some actual value.

Privity of contract

MEANING

Before we conclude this general chapter on contracts and look at standard terms in detail, it is worth spending a little time looking at a distinctive and very important common law doctrine in English law known as **'privity of contract'**. The general rule can be expressed as follows:

> A contract cannot confer rights or impose obligations on anyone who is not a party to it. It follows that, if you are not a party to a contract, you can neither sue nor be sued upon it.

A person who is not a party to a particular contract is commonly referred to as a **'third party'** to the contract.

CONSEQUENCES

While this statement of the doctrine of privity may seem utterly ordinary, its practical consequences led to the doctrine being criticized for allowing unfair and unintended or harsh consequences to arise. This was especially the case where the parties intended to confer a benefit on a third party but that party was not able to sue for that benefit.

While it is not surprising that a contract imposes no obligations on a third party, it is perhaps surprising that a contract confers no rights on a third party.

A number of exceptions to this basic rule have developed both by statute and collateral contracts. The collateral contract is a very useful tool to avoid the rule relating to privity. It is not an exception to privity because a new contract arises: it is a contract between one of the parties to an agreement with a third party relating to the same subject matter.

Validity of the contract

We have looked at what constitutes a contract and in outline at how a contract is formed. We have not so far looked at how the validity of a contract can be affected by various factors. We shall do so now briefly.

The validity of a contract may be affected by illegality, duress, undue influence, misrepresentation or mistake. The effect of these conditions make the contract either void or voidable according to the circumstances:

▶ **Voidable contracts** are contracts which are valid unless one party exercises their legal right to treat the contract as void.

▶ **Void contracts** are contracts which have no effect in law and in consequence goods or money transferred under a void contract will be recoverable.

An **illegal contract** is one where in common law it was entered into with the purpose of committing a crime, a tort (civil wrong), a fraud or a sexually immoral act, or where the contract breaches foreign law and endangers international relations or interferes in the course of justice or concerns corruption in public life. A contract is considered illegal by statute if it is prohibited either in an implied form or expressly.

Misrepresentation and mistake

Misrepresentation can be usefully defined as a false statement made by one party to induce the other contracting party to enter into the contract. The remedy in respect to misrepresentation depends on the type of misrepresentation.

The position is slightly different in respect of mistakes. Parties are usually bound regardless of mistakes. There are exceptions to this which depend on the type of mistake which occurs. If the mistake falls into that specific category, the effect on the contract is to render it void.

In respect of duress and undue influence, the general position is that the contract is voidable by the person upon whom duress or undue influence was exercised.

Conclusion

Finally, now that we have a better idea of what constitutes a contract and how important it is to focus before entering into a contract on those key elements, it is worth seeing how and when discharge of a contract or contractual agreement occurs. What is meant by **discharge** is the removal of the contractual obligations from the parties. In other words, how does the contract come to an end? The discharge of a contract arises through the following four categories:

1 performance
2 agreement
3 breach
4 frustration.

The general rule in this respect is that usually only **full performance** discharges the contract. There are, however, exceptions to this rule:

▶ The contract can be discharged by **agreement**. Again, this goes back to the basic principle of freedom of contract. The parties may agree to discharge an existing contract or for the discharge to occur once a condition has been fulfilled or an event has taken place or, conversely, for the fulfilment of a condition to activate the contract.
▶ The **breach** of certain conditions within a contract may entitle one of the contracting parties to repudiate their future obligations. In these circumstances, they would be treating the contract as discharged.
▶ The final way in which a contract can be discharged is also the most recent concept, called **frustration**. This came into being essentially under the Frustrated Contracts Act of 1943 and has been applied in case law subsequently. It deals with the discharge of contracts when, through the fault of neither party, events render the performance of the contract either physically or commercially impossible.

Now that we have looked at what makes a contract, what validates a contract and what fulfils or terminates a contract, in the next chapter we will look in more detail at standard terms and conditions.

TEST YOURSELF

1 Terms of business sent on an invoice received after the goods have been delivered will govern the transaction. True or false?

2 Within a commercial contract you can exclude liability for...

   (a) everything

   (b) nothing

   (c) everything except death and injury as long as the exclusion clause is reasonable

   (d) it doesn't matter – they will never find me in Rio de Janeiro if it all goes wrong

3 Silence from the other side can be deemed acceptance of contractual terms. True or false?

4 A legally binding contract must be in writing?

   (a) yes

   (b) no – it can include oral agreements and implied terms

   (c) sometimes

   (d) the contract is so one-sided I was surprised to see it printed on both sides of the paper

6

....

Standard terms and conditions

In this chapter you will learn about:
- *negotiating the standard terms and conditions of a contract*
- *the Unfair Contract Terms Act*
- *the main terms that form standard terms and conditions for the supply of services and goods.*

Introduction

Parties entering into an agreement will freely negotiate their own terms to suit their particular arrangement or circumstances.

Investing time in formalizing a relationship in the form of standard terms and conditions (i.e. a written contract of terms) will protect a small business by avoiding the costly risks associated with loose verbal arrangements between parties.

Negotiating standard terms and conditions

SCOPE

Standard terms and conditions can stand alone or be incorporated into the terms of the contract, where parties agree the terms of the transaction (i.e. price and quantities of goods) but use the standard terms and conditions to deal with secondary matters such as quality of goods, warranties, delivery, title and risk, payment and liabilities.

It is important to remember that, unlike with long-term supply contracts, there is no contract between two parties until the price and quantity is agreed; therefore, each time an order for particular goods is placed, a new contract is formed.

PUBLISHED TERMS

It is normal practice for parties to agree to incorporate a set of standard terms published by a particular body rather than having to endure lengthy negotiations. Please see the following professional and commercial bodies that publish standard terms and conditions for particular types of contract:

▶ The Law Society publishes standard terms and contracts for the sale of land.

▶ Lloyd's of London publishes standard terms for contracts of marine insurance.

▶ The Institute of Mechanical Engineers and the Institute of Electrical Engineers publish standard terms for contracts for mechanical and electrical engineering work.

▶ The Joint Contracts Tribunal publishes standard terms for construction contracts.

▶ The Road Haulage Association publishes standard terms for the carriage of goods by road.

Where parties use standard terms and conditions, they should ensure that they are fully aware of what is contained in them, especially where the terms are not attached to the contract that incorporates them.

Furthermore, where standard terms and conditions are not attached to the contract, it is vital to make it clear which standard terms are being incorporated. Particularly when using published terms that are updated and reissued on a regular basis, it is prudent to refer to the date, edition or reference number to which the contract refers.

In addition, where standard terms are inconsistent with terms of the contract, problems can be avoided by inserting the following:

> 'The XXX terms and conditions shall be incorporated into this contract except in so far as those terms and conditions are inconsistent with the terms negotiated between us.'

Lastly, it is advisable to all parties that they should be aware of what the terms actually mean. It is not possible to avoid contractual liability by stating that you never read, saw or understood the terms agreed.

Incorporation

Standard terms and conditions will be effective only if incorporated into the contract.

The simplest way to ensure this is done is to expressly state your intention to include a particular set of terms during pre-contract correspondence. It may be tempting to avoid expressly mentioning such terms so as to avoid the risk of the other party seeking to negotiate your terms. However, failing to do so should be balanced against the risk that the absence of an express statement will result in the terms not being fully incorporated.

As you will now be aware, contracts come into existence as a result of the acceptance of an offer. It will not be sufficient to merely insist that you always trade on the basis of your terms. The terms must be incorporated into a contractual offer and accepted on that basis in order to have full effect.

OFFER AND ACCEPTANCE

The party seeking to incorporate its own standard terms must bring those terms to the attention of the other party before the contract is made – for example, if a contract is made over the telephone and following the call the accepting party is sent the standard terms, this would be too late to incorporate the terms into the contract.

Another example is that of tickets which purport to incorporate the issuing party's standard terms and conditions. The ticket holder may receive these only after the contract has been formed. In this instance, a company could argue that their terms are incorporated by regular course of dealing – that is, as ticket holders receive tickets every time they are booked they must have taken notice of the terms and conditions. However, this argument would not be sustained if it was the first time the ticket holder booked a ticket with the issuing company. (See the discussion on course of dealing below.)

Where you are dealing with customers on a face-to-face basis, it is possible to display standard terms at the business premises. However, this approach is likely to be scrutinized by a judge, who would consider the position, size and prominence in deciding whether you brought the terms sufficiently to the customer's attention.

Therefore, the preferred way is for your business to bring the terms to the attention of the other party in as much pre-contract documentation as possible.

A supplier should make express references to its standard terms:

▶ in catalogues, brochures or other similar documents
▶ on quotations
▶ on purchase order forms
▶ on any acknowledgement or confirmation of purchase order forms
▶ on delivery notes, *and/or*
▶ on invoices.

With invoices, it is important to remember that printing standard terms on the back of an invoice will generally be ineffective; this is due to the fact that an invoice is usually not sent until much later, after the contract has been formed. However, as mentioned in the earlier example, if there is a regular course of dealing between the parties, you will be able to argue that the terms were brought to the attention of your customer over a period of time.

Where standard terms are printed on the reverse of any document, it is prudent to clearly state on the face of the document that the contract between the parties is subject to the terms on the reverse.

Furthermore, where a standard term is significantly different, you should ensure particular attention is drawn to that term.

STAFF

Where you have staff entering into contracts with clients or customers on behalf of your company, it is important to ensure that they receive the necessary guidance in how to conduct this process. For example, you should ensure that they are aware of any specific terms that they need to draw to a customer's attention.

BATTLE OF THE FORMS

A situation can occur where both contracting parties purport to rely on their own standard terms and conditions. Determining which terms will prevail is known as the '**battle of the forms**'.

To avoid this situation arising, you must always ensure that you respond to an offer, as failure to do so will mean you have accepted the other party's standard terms. In practice, this means every form of offer received from the other party has to be responded to by your form incorporating or referring to your own standard terms.

When a situation like this arises, a business can decide to discuss the conflict with the other party and agree to any variations in a side letter. This can incur time and expense for both parties; however, if you are dealing with an important customer or supplier, this can be a worthwhile exercise to encourage repeat business.

If, for any reason, both parties reject the offer they receive, there will be no contract formed. In this scenario, there is no legal framework in place to set out the basis of the transaction; therefore, the only obligation the courts will impose will be for the customer to pay a reasonable price for any goods or services they actually received. This is known as a **'quantum meruit' payment,** meaning 'for what it's worth'. Be aware that this is not always the price agreed by the parties.

COURSE OF DEALING

Where you are unable to incorporate standard terms by express agreement from the other party or through the battle of the forms, it may be possible to convince the other party that the standard terms are incorporated as part of a course of dealing between the parties (i.e. as a result of their consistent use in previous transactions). To establish this, you must show:

▶ regular trading between the parties, preferably several transactions per month over a period of years (however, three or four transactions over a period of several years is unlikely to be sufficient), *and/or*
▶ that trading has been consistent – i.e. that trading was on the same terms and a consistent procedure was followed.

This way of incorporating standard terms should always be seen as a last resort as there is a large degree of uncertainty in how the courts approach this situation.

The Unfair Contract Terms Act

Transactions between businesses are covered by the Unfair Contract Terms Act 1977 (UCTA). The Act specifically applies where one party is dealing on his/her own written standard terms of business and not where the parties have negotiated a set of terms.

UCTA places restrictions on businesses that seek to use standard terms to achieve a contractual advantage as follows:

Where one party is conducting business on his/her own written standard terms, the following terms are ineffective unless reasonable:

▶ a term which excludes/restricts liability for breach of contract (e.g. losses caused by negligence, defective or poor-quality goods)
▶ a term which allows a party to render a contractual performance different from that which was reasonably expected of him/her
▶ a term which allows a party to render no performance at all for the whole or any part of his/her contractual obligation.

Under any circumstances, you cannot exclude liability for death or injury.

When determining what is 'reasonable', the court will take into account:

▶ the information available to both parties when the contract was drawn up
▶ whether the contract was negotiated or in standard form, *and*
▶ whether the buyer had the bargaining power to negotiate better terms.

Main terms

Table 6.1 shows the main terms that form standard terms and conditions for the supply of services and goods.

Table 6.1 *Main terms that form standard terms and conditions for the supply of services and goods*

Supply of services	Supply of goods
Description of services	Description and specification
Order forms	Order forms
Obligation to provide services	Quantity
Standard of services	Quality
Transferred goods	Acceptance
Deliverables	Delivery
Time for performance of services	Price
Intellectual property rights	Payment
Charges	Packaging
Payment	Risk
	Title

Boilerplate terms:
Force majeure
Entire agreement

It is important to consider the practical implications any clause will have on the day-to-day running of your business. We will look at a few examples to get a feel for how these clauses may look or be varied. However, you will need to seek legal advice when drafting a form of standard terms and conditions that will suit you.

TIME FOR PERFORMANCE OF SERVICES

This term should be expressly stated in any contract, setting out when work is to begin, a completion date and the process by which completion is determined.

As a supplier you will want to try to limit your obligation for performance times to allow flexibility. This can be done by including the qualification that you will do your best or make all reasonable endeavours to meet certain dates. It would also be worthwhile trying to limit your liability for any breach of this obligation.

In contrast, a customer may want to expressly state that a supplier starts services by a definite date and performs obligations by a specific completion date. A customer is also likely to want to be able to terminate a contract for a supplier's failure to meet a completion date.

If there is no express date in a contract and no previous course of dealings between the parties, there is an implied term that the supplier will carry out the service within a reasonable time. Assessing what is reasonable is fact based, is problematic and causes uncertainty.

Pro-supplier clause:
'The Supplier shall have the right to make any changes to the Services which are necessary to comply with any applicable law or safety requirement, or which do not materially affect the nature or quality of the Services, and the Supplier shall notify the Customer in any such event. The Supplier warrants to the Customer that the Services will be provided using reasonable care and skill.'

Pro-customer clause:

'The Supplier shall from [the Commencement Date OR the date set in the Order] and for the duration of this Contract provide the Services to the Customer in accordance with the terms of the Contract. The Supplier shall meet any performance dates for the Services specified in the [Order] or notified to the Supplier by the Customer.'

ENTIRE AGREEMENT

An entire agreement clause (an example is given below) seeks to ensure that the contractual relationship is governed by one document setting out the agreements reached between the parties and to exclude liability for statements or representations made by a supplier's staff or in its sales brochures and catalogues.

'The Contract constitutes the entire agreement between the parties. The Customer acknowledges that it has not relied on any statement, promise or representation made or given by or on behalf of the Supplier which is not set out in the Contract.'

It is, however, important to remember that entire agreement clauses are not always effective.

RISK

Risk and title are tied together in that when title of goods passes from the supplier to the customer, so does the risk. In light of this, it is necessary to be aware that, where goods are destroyed before the risk passes to the customer, a supplier is liable to provide the customer with the equivalent quantity of goods. The converse is also true that, if the goods are destroyed after risk has passed to the customer, the customer is still liable for the price of the goods.

Suppliers should be clear about when they want risk to transfer – for example, when the goods leave their premises, when the goods are delivered to the customer, or (where they have a commercially aggressive customer) when payment is made. The first scenario is the most supplier-friendly solution.

However, if risk is to pass on delivery, the supplier should require the customer to insure the goods from delivery against all risks. This will protect the supplier where goods are destroyed or the customer is unable to pay for the goods.

> **Example risk clause:**
> 'The risk in the Goods shall pass to the Customer on completion of delivery.'

Conclusion

This chapter has looked in general at the key components of standard terms and conditions. It highlights the main issues to be aware of when contracting with suppliers or customers in your business. Here is a brief outline that serves as a reminder of the points we have considered:

- ► The central principle of a contract is freedom of contract.
- ► The contract represents an agreement which the parties intend to legally bind each other.
- ► The contract depicts the relationship and sets out the parties' intention.
- ► The contract should not be an afterthought as it is central to defining the very foundation of the business.

It is always worth spending time to review your contracts, ensuring that, where you have concerns or things are unclear, you seek legal advice to understand the overall terms and structure. The downside of not doing so can have significant financial consequences, which are often disastrous for both small and large businesses.

TEST YOURSELF

1 Your business prints its standard terms and conditions on the back of the invoice sent when orders are delivered. This is...

   (a) an effective way to incorporate your terms and conditions as invoices will always be sent

   (b) rather foolish as the contract is formed when there is an offer and acceptance which happens at the point an order is submitted and therefore terms sent out after this are not legally enforceable as they are not incorporated into the contract between the parties

   (c) a waste of time as no one reads them

   (d) a negligence claim waiting to happen against your old solicitors

2 The battle of the forms is...

   (a) the term for describing which set of terms and conditions was sent before the contract was concluded

   (b) an avant-garde sculpture movement

   (c) a discussion about the relative merits of different models.

3 You can never exclude liability for death or personal injury in your terms and conditions. True or false?

4 Your company, The Really Chilled Food Co. Ltd, supplies one of its core products, Cool Beans, to the Super-Hot Hotel Group. One of the delivery lorries crashes en route to the hotel and all the Cool Beans are destroyed. You want the Super-Hot Hotel Group to pay for a new delivery as the Cool Beans had left the factory and so were not your responsibility. This depends on...

   (a) what the terms and conditions say about when title and risk in the Cool Beans transferred

   (b) who instructs the most aggressive lawyers

   (c) No idea because I haven't read the last chapter and am just skipping to the questions as they seem rather good

Cash, funding and debt recovery

In this chapter you will learn:
- *how to protect your company and cash flow against unpaid debt*
- *the importance of knowing your customers*
- *how to develop a successful credit policy*
- *how to establish whether your debtor can pay and developing a strategy for successful enforcement*
- *what to do as a last resort.*

Cash flow

Cash flow is the lifeblood of any business, whether it is cash out to your creditors to cover stock, rent and other business expenses, or cash in as payment from your debtors to cover goods or services that you have provided to them. This will include your profit.

It is therefore vital that you ensure any documentation you use is clear and concise and is presented in a professional manner. That will include any contracts for goods or services provided, any pro forma invoices or purchase orders, and the actual invoice itself.

By the time the invoice has been raised, you should be entirely clear as to what has been agreed and the timing of any payment that you expect to receive. It may be worth getting a solicitor to check that your documentation is correct and contains any claw-back or retention clauses that would be sensible. We dealt previously with the formation of a legally binding contract in (see Chapters 5 and 6).

Prior to actually committing to doing business with somebody, you need to ensure that, if payment is not to be made prior to the goods being manufactured or supplied, they will indeed be good for the money when it becomes due. You can best protect your position by getting trade references through one of the established agencies, seeking references from other customers, taking a deposit or asking for up-to-date accounting information or bank statements, though these are not sure-fire guarantees. You may also look to take out an 'indemnity insurance' – this can usually protect up to 85 per cent of the net invoice and will attract a premium of between 1 and 4 per cent. If you do not do all or any of this, with the best will in the world, you face the possibility of a debt going bad.

Factoring or invoice discounting

Many companies also look at the options of working with a **factoring** or **invoice discounting company**. In essence, these are specialist finance providers that use the contract with your clients and the debt that comes from this to provide lines of credit. This can be very useful for fast-growing businesses or where funds from banks in the traditional sense may not be available or will not be substantial enough. Typically, they will lend up to 70 per cent of the net invoice value and will assist in client vetting, invoice and credit collection management, as well as providing insurance to cover the debt at extra cost. In simple terms, **factoring** is used by smaller companies who may have limited bookkeeping and accountancy resources internally, whereas **invoice discounting** leaves greater control to the company itself and is generally available only to larger concerns.

If companies are engaged in the supply of imported goods, they can also look at trade finance. This is where a funder provides a line of credit or specific advances against an agreed purchase order (the typical cost is 2 to 4 per cent of the purchase order) but again is a safe and beneficial way of dealing with this type of supply.

Never underestimate the importance of good accounting systems, clear credit vetting of clients and the use of professional providers to assist and protect your cash flow – and deal with the consequences if it goes wrong.

What is a commercial debt?

A commercial debt is a debt that arises out of a contract for the supply of goods and/or services made between all businesses and public sector bodies. All businesses no matter how big or small have been able, since 7 August 2002, to claim late payment interest under the Late Payment of Commercial Debts (Interest) Act 1998. This is a higher rate of interest and is discussed in more detail later on in this chapter. Contracts with consumers are not covered by this Act – for the Act to apply, either party may be a sole trader, registered company, partnership, public organization, body corporate, trust or other legal entity, as long as both contracting parties are engaged in business activity via a contract.

Know your customer

It is very important that you know, from the outset, whom you are dealing with. Ensure that you get proper terms of business drawn up before entering into a legally binding relationship with the customer. Your terms should clearly state that you will utilize credit reference agencies, and ensure that you follow this up and perform a credit reference check on your customer *before* entering into a contract with them. You should obtain a signed authority from your proposed customer which provides you with their permission to undertake a credit check on them. If your customer is going to be a company, ensure that you know who the directors of the company are. If the customer is a sole trader, make sure you obtain their home address. It is very important to make your payment terms clear so that there cannot be any doubt in the customer's mind. Where your customer is a company, use a credit reference agency to ensure that the company is solvent; if the company is insolvent, then obtain a guarantee from one or more of the company's directors. Above all, it is extremely important that you have an effective credit control system in place. You will learn more about credit control later on in this chapter.

If you are required to sue a customer for an unpaid debt and you obtain a judgment against your customer, one of the most common reasons why a judgment cannot be enforced is because the claim was brought against the wrong entity. For example, you are owed money by 'A Limited trading as Firm B' and you sue Firm B (i.e. the trading name); what you should have done was sue 'A Limited trading as Firm B'.

So, it is essential to find out who your customer is before you start recovery action against them and this is best done at the outset of your relationship with your customer. Here are some helpful tips:

Individuals and sole traders

▶ Ensure that you get the customer's name 100-per-cent accurate – even a small mistake (for example, a spelling mistake) could prevent successful recovery.

Sole traders and partnerships 'trading as'

▶ Ensure that you obtain the name of the entity they are trading as, as well as the name of every single individual running or involved with the business on a management level. This will enable you to enforce a judgment against the assets of the trading entity or, if it has no assets, or has ceased trading, the individuals' personal assets.

Partnerships

▶ Apart from limited liability partnerships (LLPs), partnerships are not legal entities but are a collection of individuals who trade together. Therefore, the partners themselves are liable for any debts incurred by the business. It is for that reason very important you obtain the full names of all the partners at the outset of your relationship with them.

Limited companies

▶ Check at Companies House (www.companieshouse.gov.uk) that you have taken the company's name down accurately. You can also check the registered office details. If you are seeking to recover a debt from a limited company, ensure that you are going after the company which you actually did business with. For example, if an order was placed by Company (World) Limited, make sure you don't sue Company (UK) Limited. This is the case even if both companies have the same directors. As mentioned above, often a limited company can be 'trading as' another name. This is frequently the case with restaurants. If you cannot establish which limited company is behind the trading name, then, using the example above, you should sue 'Firm B'.

As stated above, it is very important that you run credit checks on your potential customer and ensure that you run those checks on the correct individual/entity. Knowing whom to pursue when things go wrong is key. You might also want to consider setting a credit limit for your customer – if you do, make sure that you stick to that limit. If credit limits are put in place, it is sensible to review them often. You should also keep a close eye on your customer's payment history so that if things do go wrong, you will be the first in the line of creditors. If a limited company has a parent company (i.e. you are dealing with part of a group of companies), it is worth considering obtaining a guarantee from the parent company so that, if you have problems with the subsidiary company, you can look to recover outstanding monies from the parent company.

Develop a successful credit policy

What are you hoping to achieve by recovering an outstanding debt? Answer 'yes' or 'no' to these three questions:

1 Do you want to recover the cash from your debtor?
2 Do you want simply to achieve a paper judgment against your debtor?
3 Do you want to litigate based on a principle?

You should always answer 'yes' to the first question and 'no' to the other two questions – in other words, you should always want to recover the money owed from your debtor. If you are able to develop a strategy to enforce any judgment which results, this means you are not litigating on a principle and you do not just want to obtain the paper judgment. Litigating on a principle will almost always end up as an extremely shallow victory for you and probably not one which you wish to promote as an organization.

You should not leave a debt outstanding for more than a few months in the hope that the process of litigation will prove to be your panacea for a successful recovery when you reach that point in your credit control process. Always bear in mind that time is of the essence in debt recovery. Your credit control process should not leave litigation as a last resort, with everything being left to the initial collection process. Some of your customers will pay on time and promptly following receipt of your invoice. Others will pay within your standard payment terms. However, you need to accept that some debtors are only ever going to pay you once they are pushed, and therefore what you need to do is use litigation within your collection process as an escalation tool and as a threat. Don't leave litigation at the bottom of the pile. Remember that when you are convincing these tricky customers to part with their cash, you are in competition for their money with your customer's other creditors. You therefore need to sell to your customer the benefit of paying off the debt.

Bear in mind also that a debt which reaches litigation has a smaller chance of recovery and it is important that you are realistic about the prospects of recovery when you go down this route. The biggest problem you are likely to face is enforcing any judgment you obtain against your 'won't pay' debtors, and it may be that you will need to make a commercial decision about how far to pursue enforcement options. Try not to throw good money after bad.

You should have a credit policy in place; this will help to reduce the likelihood of irrecoverable debt. Credit policies deal with the risks and costs involved in extending credit to customers. Such a policy will also underline the importance to your organization of maintaining a positive cash flow. The policy needs to be clearly understood by members of your organization, clearly defined and implemented constantly when you are contracting with clients.

You will need to develop a range of reliable search procedures which will verify the information given by the customer when they apply for credit. Remember that in a lending environment it is extremely important to obtain an independent (and reliable) assessment of a prospective customer's credit rating before opening an account for them. The information can thereafter be updated periodically by obtaining reports from a credit reference agency (for example, Equifax or Experian).

A good credit policy will set out the terms upon which you will extend credit to customers, including as a minimum:

▶ **The steps which will be taken to assess a customer for credit –**
  ▷ define the information to be given by customers as part of their application for credit
  ▷ look into the appropriate authorities for establishing high-risk accounts (e.g. overseas students with assets outside England and Wales)
  ▷ evaluate the information given to you by customers to assess risk and potential methods of enforcement should they default

- ▶ **How credit will be granted to the customer –**
  - ▷ define the level below which credit accounts will not be opened
  - ▷ set out who must authorize the opening of accounts
  - ▷ set out the documentation and procedures adopted for opening an account
  - ▷ confirm standard payment terms
  - ▷ confirm levels at which special payment terms might be negotiated (if appropriate)
  - ▷ set out your procedures for confirming that an account has been opened and advising the customer of the credit limit
- ▶ **What your collection policy is –**
  - ▷ what the process of collection will be and how it will be used
  - ▷ the collection timescale and the timescale for passing accounts to action
  - ▷ a process for the resolution of customer queries
  - ▷ depending on the debtor's circumstances, the commercial sanctions to be used (which can include outsourcing the matter to a debt collection agent or in-house litigation)
- ▶ **What your policy is where a customer is made insolvent –**
  - ▷ you will need to cover the different types of insolvency (e.g. a customer who is a discharged bankrupt, a customer who is entering into an IVA, etc.).

The credit policy should ideally be contained in a written document. You will also need to draw up a credit application form. In that form, you will need to ask questions of the customer and ensure that you are happy with the customer's answers before extending credit to them.

What happens when an account goes into default?

Your collection process is likely to start off with a series of letters being sent to defaulting customers. Those letters will remind them that there is a balance due from them and will encourage them to pay. You should bear in mind that letter cycles should not include too many letters; a statement and two or three letters is plenty and, if you send many more letters than that, it is likely that your words will fall on deaf ears. It is very important, where you have customers who regularly default, to change the dispatch dates of letters often, as well as the wording of letters to avoid complacency among regular defaulters. Letters tend to have an immediate effect on a reader and it is important that you are positive in your letter – if you are not, it is likely that your letter will be binned. Hopefully, your letter will encourage the debtor to take matters seriously and do something about it.

There are some simple rules to bear in mind when drafting your debt-collection letter in order that it grabs the attention of the reader:

▶ Make sure you send the letter to the correct address and with the correct name. If you do not, you are probably asking for payment problems. If you are writing to a group of companies and send the letter to the wrong address, the company is likely to write to you asking for the correct details and this will delay matters further. It is a good idea to address your letters to the financial director of the company. If you know his/her name, state it and, if not, simply state 'Financial Director' and mark the envelope 'private and confidential'. This usually means that it is opened by the financial director himself/herself, rather than by a secretary or somebody in the post room.

▶ Remind your customer of your payment terms.

▶ Make your letter look good and eye-catching. Use a modern layout and use good-quality paper. Check and double-check for spelling mistakes. If you do not make the effort with your letter, it is likely the recipient will not bother to read it.

▶ Make sure you show the amount that is owed clearly, in figures. That way there can be no doubt as to what is owed. Try and state reference or invoice numbers to make it easier for your customer.

▶ To avoid misunderstandings about when payment is due, specify the date by which you must receive the overdue payment.

▶ You need to spell out to your customer what the consequences will be if payment is not forthcoming by the relevant date. However, you need to be sure that you can (and will) follow through with the threat. It is not worth making empty threats. You could say that you will 'consider' court action, for example, and that will give you a way out if you decide you do not wish to sue the customer.

- ▶ Allow for the possibility that the customer's payment has crossed in the post with your letter. Politely tell your customer to ignore the letter if their payment has been sent in the last few days.
- ▶ Sign your letter yourself. This will make a much better impression on a debtor than a letter that has been 'pp'd'.

Other initial methods to consider when contacting debtors are text messages, emails and visiting your customer personally. If you decide to do the latter, you may wish to think about whether the visit can also be used as an opportunity to collect information which you can later use in litigation or enforcement (for example, make a mental note of what fixed assets there are on the premises).

You can also try telephoning your debtors and this is often a very effective way of collecting your outstanding debts. Consider these points about telephone collections:

- ▶ Use your customer's name at the beginning of the call and throughout. People listen closely when their name is being used.
- ▶ Ensure that you know the facts before you make the call – how much is the debt worth, what are the payment methods, etc.
- ▶ Keep a record of when you have called your debtors and make a note of what was said.
- ▶ If you tell your debtor you will do something, make sure you do it.
- ▶ Make a diary note to follow up the telephone call.
- ▶ Try and get your debtor to promise to make a payment today, or at least a commitment from them to do something.
- ▶ Stay in control and remain confident, positive and persistent. Ensure that you are always polite.
- ▶ Use the conversation with the debtor to obtain information which may help you later on in the collection process.
- ▶ Make sure you close the call properly. Confirm the amount that will be paid, the date it will be paid and use the debtor's name once more to finish the call.

LATE PAYMENT OF COMMERCIAL DEBTS (INTEREST) ACT 1998

As was mentioned above, businesses can add interest onto an overdue debt under this Act where both parties are trading in the course of business. This is unless contractual interest has been agreed between the parties. The current rate of interest under the Act is 8.5 per cent.

A creditor can also claim fixed compensation, the level of which is based on the value of the debt, as follows:

Less than £1,000.00	£40.00
£1,000.00 *to* £10,000.00	£70.00
£10,000.00 *or more*	£100.00

The Act can help you because:

▶ where there is no contractual right to interest, the Act gives businesses the legal right to claim interest on their overdue commercial debts, *and*
▶ it allows the creditor business to claim compensation for reasonable debt recovery costs.

Delaying tactics

Inevitably, some debtors will try to use delaying tactics to avoid having to pay you there and then; they will come up with all sorts of reasons why they cannot pay you today. In order to try and overcome these you need to try to take away the reason for the debtor not to pay you, remain confident and create a mood of co-operation with your debtor.

Some examples of delaying tactics are:

▶ 'I can't afford to pay' – if you believe this, then try and agree with your debtor that they will pay in instalments, even if they are small instalments to begin with.
▶ 'I'm afraid he is not available' – contact the debtor again and again.
▶ 'Please could we have a copy of the statement' – when you have already sent the statement several times.
▶ 'I will pay you as soon as we end this call' – try to appeal to the debtor's sense of honour and say something like 'I have your word on that' at the end of the call.
▶ The debtor sends you a cheque which is not made out correctly.

Can your debtor pay?

Before deciding whether to take recovery action and before you decide how much you wish to invest in recovery action, you should check the financial status of your debtor. If you are able to obtain a good knowledge of the debtor's assets, you will be able to assess potential risks (such as the debtor getting rid of those assets) and take any necessary preventative action (e.g. an injunction).

There are various checks you can make, for example:

▶ **Tracing agents** – a tracing agent will have access to databases which are not publicly available and can therefore find out some fairly detailed information about the debtor. A tracing agent can be engaged to check whether the debtor has other residences, what assets the debtor has, what vehicles are owned by the debtor, phone records, whether the debtor holds any company shares, etc.
▶ **Public records** – these are simple checks and include:
  ▷ The Insolvency Service website (www.insolvency.gov.uk) – to check whether sole traders and individuals are bankrupt.
  ▷ Companies House website (www.companieshouse.gov.uk) – to check that the company continues to trade. You can also obtain accounts for previous years.
  ▷ Land Registry website (www.landregistry.gov.uk) – can be used to check whether the debtor owns any property or land.
▶ **Credit reference agencies** – these will provide you with up-to-date credit scores and financial information.
▶ **Registry Trust** – you can use this to check whether the debtor has any other judgments registered against him/her www.trustonline.org.uk.
▶ **www.192.com, Royal Mail and Yellow Pages websites** – to check your customer's current address and the accuracy of any address you may have for the customer.
▶ **www.google.co.uk** – it is sometimes worth Googling your customer to find out more information about them.
▶ **Oral examination** – this can only take place once judgment has been obtained against a debtor but can be a very useful tool for a creditor. The creditor makes an application to the court for the debtor to attend court to provide information about the debtor's assets, etc., to the creditor.

Once you have obtained a better idea about the assets your debtor has, you can look at the assets and consider whether it is worth litigating against that particular customer in terms of whether the debtor has any assets which you may be able to enforce against in due course. You may also need to go back to the customer's credit application form, notes of conversations and correspondence to look further into the assets available.

Consider the following:

▶ In the case of an individual or a sole trader operating from home, are there goods in their home which you may be able to seize?
▶ Is the home in their name?
▶ If an individual is employed, could you obtain an attachment of earnings order against them so that some of their salary goes to you?
▶ Does the debtor have a bank account so that you can obtain a third-party debt order?

If you are unable to locate your customer, it is likely that you will need to use a tracing agent (as above) in any case. If none of the investigations you make prove to be successful, then ensure that you choose a reputable tracing agent to make further enquiries for you, and in particular try and choose one which takes data protection obligations seriously. You are ultimately responsible for the tracing agent's actions.

Debtors abroad

Sometimes you will have debtors who live outside England and Wales and therefore fall outside the jurisdiction of the courts of England and Wales. Your credit policy should therefore include provisions for what to do when a debtor is outside England and Wales.

The jurisdiction of the courts of England and Wales includes 'any part of the territorial waters of the United Kingdom adjoining England and Wales', which includes the Scilly Isles and the Isle of Wight but does not include the Channel Islands, Ireland, Northern Ireland, Scotland or the Isle of Man.

Regulatory environment

Debt recovery is the subject of various pieces of legislation and you need to bear in mind:

▶ the Data Protection Act
▶ the Human Rights Act
▶ the Limitation Act
▶ the Administration of Justice Act
▶ the Business Names Act
▶ the Office of Fair Trading's Debt Collection Guidance.

Last resort

If your usual methods of debt recovery are unsuccessful, then you will probably want to consider litigation as a last resort.

You will need to consider:

- ▶ whether you are likely to win your claim and whether it will be disputed
- ▶ whether Alternative Dispute Resolution is appropriate, particularly if you do not want to damage the relationship you have with the customer
- ▶ whether you are likely to recover any money
- ▶ whether you have the time to litigate
- ▶ whether you can afford to litigate
- ▶ whether the debtor has any other judgments against him/her – if so, it may be less likely that you will recover your money.

TEST YOURSELF

1 In order to reduce the risk of unpaid debts, you should...

   (a) avoid going into business

   (b) get payment upfront where possible

   (c) undertake appropriate credit checks and due diligence before extending credit to customers

   (d) invest in a baseball bat

2 An oral examination is...

   (a) something that your dentist carries out every six months

   (b) an application to the court once judgment has been obtained in a debt claim to enable you to question the debtor about their assets and ability to pay the debt

   (c) something that you have in A level French

   (d) make up your own joke

3 If a debtor has a job, then you can...

   (a) seek an attachment of earnings order requiring their employer to pay part of their salary direct to you to satisfy the debt

   (b) force their employer to dismiss them

   (c) arrange a public flogging at which you get first crack of the whip

8

Dispute resolution

In this chapter you will learn about:
- *limitation periods and why they are important*
- *the 'without prejudice' rule*
- *the importance of evidence in disputes*
- *finalizing settlement agreements*
- *mediation and how it is practised in the UK.*

Why limitation periods are important

YOU COULD LOSE THE RIGHT TO BRING A CLAIM

The Limitation Act 1980 sets out limitation periods for different types of claim, several of which are set out in Table 8.1 below. Formal proceedings must be issued within the relevant period or the defendant to a claim will have an absolute defence, regardless of the strength of the claim. It is therefore imperative that a claimant does not delay or allow settlement negotiations to run on beyond a limitation period without issuing proceedings before expiry of the limitation period.

The limitation period can be stayed (suspended) by agreement between the parties. Any such agreement should be finalized and recorded in writing well before the expiry of the limitation period. A defendant to a claim does not have to agree to a standstill of the limitation period. In the absence of an agreement, the claimant should issue proceedings before expiry of the relevant period. Either party to the litigation could then seek a stay of proceedings to enable settlement negotiations to take place (or continue) if appropriate.

Table 8.1   Some examples of limitation periods for common types of claim

Type of action	Starting event	Period
Simple contract	Accrual of cause of action (the date of breach of contract)	6 years
Tort (other than for personal injuries, under the Consumer Protection Act 1987, for latent damage, or for defamation)	Accrual of cause of action (the date the damage is suffered)	6 years
Personal injury or death	The later of: accrual of cause of action, *or* date of knowledge of the person injured	3 years The court may disapply this limit if it would be just to do so.
Defamation or malicious prosecution	Accrual of cause of action	1 year The court may disapply this limit if it would be just to do so.
Informal loan contracts	Accrual of cause of action (the date of written demand for repayment)	6 years
'Speciality', such as documents under seal/deeds	Accrual of cause of action (the date of breach of contract)	12 years
Action for contribution	The date of judgment or settlement	2 years
Latent damage other than personal injury (in the tort of negligence)	The later of: accrual of cause of action, *or* the date when the claimant first had the knowledge required for bringing the action and the right to bring such an action.	6 years 3 years (personal injury) Overriding time limit: 15 years (section 14B, Limitation Act)

(*continued*)

Table 8.1 Some examples of limitation periods for common types of claim (continued)

Postponement of limitation period in the case of fraud	Time will start to run when the fraud is discovered by the claimant, or when the claimant could, with reasonable diligence have discovered it.	N/A
Action against a company which goes into liquidation	N/A	Time stops running for limitation purposes. For compulsory liquidation, time stops running on the making of a winding-up order. For voluntary liquidation, time stops running from the company passing a resolution to put the company into liquidation.
Action against a company which goes into administration	N/A	Time does not stop running for limitation purposes.
Judicial review	The date when the grounds for the application first arose (usually the date of a relevant decision)	Promptly and, in any event, within 3 months

YOU COULD LOSE THE RIGHT TO AMEND CLAIMS IN EXISTING PROCEEDINGS

If the limitation period has expired, this could affect a claimant's ability, in existing proceedings, to add new parties or claims.

YOU COULD RECOVER LESS DAMAGES

There are different time limits for contract and non-contractual claims. A claim based on a simple contract has a limitation period of six years from the accrual of the cause of action (as opposed to 12 years for an agreement executed as a deed). The cause of action in a contract accrues at the date of the breach of contract, regardless of whether any loss has in fact been suffered at that time. A non-contractual claim in tort generally has a six-year period from accrual of the cause of action. However, a cause of action in tort does not accrue until damage has been suffered, which may be much later than when a breach of contract occurred.

If a claimant misses the contractual limitation period, he/she may still be able to sue in tort, but the level of damages recoverable in tort is generally less than the damages recoverable for a contract claim.

A party to a settlement has two years from the date of settlement to seek an indemnity or contribution to the losses suffered from a third party. If proceedings are not issued against that third party in time, the right to claim from them will be lost.

When does the limitation period start?

The limitation period usually starts from the date when the right to bring the claim has arisen. As noted above, this is six years from breach of contract, and six years from the date when damage was suffered in a tort claim. Claims in respect of personal injury or death have a limitation period of three years, and defamation has a one-year limitation period from the time the cause of action accrued.

In some cases, a claimant will not know that he/she has a cause of action until he/she is aware of all the relevant facts. This could be because the defendant has deliberately concealed material facts from the claimant, or simply that the claimant was unaware of facts which give rise to the right to bring a claim.

The starting event can be postponed to the time when the claimant was aware, or ought reasonably to have been aware, of the necessary relevant facts. This only applies to claims for fraud or based on mistake, personal injury claims, deliberate concealment of facts by the defendant, or tort claims where the damage is latent (i.e. not apparent for some time).

What is 'without prejudice' privilege?

Common sense and the court procedural rules encourage parties to a dispute to settle their differences by negotiation rather than by formal proceedings. But it is understandable that parties would be reluctant to speak freely, and make concessions in negotiations that may help lead to a settlement, if those concessions could be used against them in court or other formal proceedings.

The **'without prejudice rule'** generally prevents a written or oral statement made by a party against his/her interest – or matters disclosed or addressed in without prejudice communications, in a genuine attempt to settle a dispute – from being used in a court or tribunal as evidence of an admission. There are some limited exceptions, which are referred to below.

Without prejudice privilege will only apply if:

▶ there is a dispute, *and*
▶ the statements are made in a genuine attempt to settle the dispute.

Court proceedings do not have to have started, or even be contemplated, for there to be a 'dispute' to which the rule can apply. In broad terms, there is likely to be a dispute if litigation may follow if a settlement is not reached.

Is there a dispute for the purposes of the rule? – examples

Company A and Company B are negotiating a contract for the supply of materials. They cannot agree on certain terms (e.g. price).

No dispute. This is a pre-contract commercial negotiation. A failure to agree will result in no contract rather than litigation. Concessions made in these negotiations will not be covered by the rule.

Company A and Company B have a contract for the supply of materials. Company B complains about the quality and about late delivery and seeks redress. Company A denies the allegations.

This will be a dispute for the purposes of the rule. If there is no settlement of the dispute, formal proceedings may follow. Settlement negotiations should be covered by the rule.

SHOULD I LABEL ALL COMMUNICATIONS 'WITHOUT PREJUDICE'?

If a court has to consider whether a document is protected by the without prejudice rule, it will objectively consider the document and the background circumstances, rather than its form. A failure to label a document 'without prejudice' will not mean that it is not protected by the rule if it was created in a genuine attempt to settle a dispute. Similarly, the fact that a document is described as being 'without prejudice' will not bring it within the rule if it was not made in a genuine attempt to settle a dispute.

As a matter of prudence, one should normally label a document 'without prejudice' where appropriate to reduce the scope for argument as to whether the rule applies.

If meetings or conversations are to be 'without prejudice', so that the discussions should not be admitted as evidence in formal proceedings, this should ideally (a) be agreed with the other party or parties in advance, and (b) recorded in writing.

EXCEPTIONS TO THE RULE

There are certain exceptions to the rule that without prejudice material is not allowed to be used in proceedings. The most common exceptions include the following:

- ▶ If there is a dispute as to whether a settlement was reached following without prejudice negotiations, the without prejudice material can be reviewed by a court to see if a settlement was in fact reached.
- ▶ Without prejudice material can also be used in some circumstances if there is an issue as to the interpretation of a settlement agreement.
- ▶ It can be used as evidence of the reasonableness of a settlement – that is, to demonstrate to another party or tribunal that reasonable steps had been taken to mitigate a loss.
- ▶ Where a party has made offers to settle 'without prejudice save as to costs', those offers can be shown to the court when it is considering what costs orders to make.
- ▶ It can be used as evidence of misrepresentation, undue influence, fraud, perjury, blackmail or other 'unambiguous impropriety'.

The importance of evidence in disputes

Disputes are often won or lost by reference to evidence, or the lack of it. The general rule in civil litigation is that a person who is asserting a fact must prove it on a 'balance of probabilities'. This means that a party asserting a fact or event must persuade a court that their version of events is more likely than not to have occurred.

A failure to produce relevant evidence can result in a dispute, or part of a dispute, being lost. Over time, documents get destroyed or mislaid, witnesses' memories fade and witnesses may no longer be readily available (for example, if they have died, moved or fallen out with one of the parties). It is therefore important to secure evidence as soon as a dispute arises, when memories are fresh and documents are still available.

The quality of evidence available will also help you or your lawyers assess the strengths and weaknesses of your case, and could be invaluable in settlement negotiations before trial. It is essential that you do not hide facts or evidence from your lawyers. They will need the full picture to advise you properly, including how to deal with any evidence which may be damaging to your case. Details of discussions and correspondence between a client and his/her lawyer do not (save in very exceptional circumstances, such as involvement in procuring a fraud) have to be disclosed to an opposing party.

Types of evidence to be secured

WITNESS EVIDENCE

Ideally, a **written witness statement** should be obtained from all those whose evidence may be relevant as soon as possible. The statement should set out the witness's recollection of facts and events within that person's knowledge, by reference to relevant documents where appropriate. The statement should be signed and dated, and give the witness's address and occupation. If further issues arise and need to be addressed later before the trial, it may be possible, if the witness is still available, to revise his/her statement or provide a supplemental statement. A shorter witness statement might later be prepared if the issues that need to be addressed have narrowed. If a witness has died or become hostile before a statement is obtained, valuable evidence may have been lost.

The detail in a witness statement will vary depending on the issues involved in the dispute. For example, a statement of a witness to an oral agreement between party A and party B might only need state that he/she witnessed the agreement being made, between A and B, when and where the agreement was made and the terms agreed. For a more complex dispute with many facts and issues, a more comprehensive statement would be required.

There is no 'property' in a witness, so a party is free to approach anyone to provide a statement. Whether they are willing or able to provide a statement is another matter – but if you do not ask, you will not find out.

Courts are often faced with witnesses whose stories differ. In these circumstances, a judge will have to assess the credibility of the witnesses and decide whose evidence he/she prefers. In reaching his/her decision, the judge will take into account not only how the witness gave evidence, but also what other evidence there is (e.g. documents or other witnesses' evidence) to support or damage the witness's credibility. The Court of Appeal has stated:

> **Contemporaneous written documentation is of the very greatest importance in assessing credibility. Moreover, it can be significant not only where it is present and the oral evidence can then be checked against it. It can also be significant if written documentation is absent.**

Discrepancies between what a witness says and what other witnesses or documents say should be investigated and cleared so far as possible at an early stage.

DOCUMENTS

All documents (including electronic documents such as emails, drafts of documents and video evidence) which may relate in any way to a dispute should be retained, and not altered, amended or destroyed, as soon as a dispute arises. This is to ensure that evidence is secured at an early stage, and that all relevant documents may be disclosed and protected in due course in litigation. If a party has failed to preserve relevant evidence, a judge may draw adverse inferences against that party, particularly if the documents were altered or destroyed after a dispute had started or it was apparent that a dispute was likely.

Once a dispute seems likely, all personnel should be told not to destroy or amend documents which might be relevant to the dispute. Systems in place for routine destruction or deletion of hard copy or electronic documents, by the organization and all relevant employees, should be overridden to ensure that potentially relevant documents are not destroyed.

Issues in a dispute may develop or change over time. If you have any doubt as to whether a document might be relevant to issues in a dispute, make sure it is retained.

Documents in the possession of third parties should be obtained as soon as possible. These may include official records such as police reports, accident report books, or other documents in the hands of third parties. If the third party is unwilling to provide information voluntarily, consider making a subject access request under the Data Protection Act or a Freedom of Information Act request. Where proceedings have been issued, and in some circumstances before proceedings have been issued, a third party can be ordered by the court to produce relevant documents.

'REAL' EVIDENCE

When lawyers refer to 'real' evidence, this is generally to describe evidence other than witness statements and documents. This may include, for example, the goods or products which are the subject of the dispute. This evidence should be retained, unaltered, so that it is available for the trial and for inspection by experts, if appropriate.

OTHER CONTEMPORANEOUS EVIDENCE

Relevant photographs and measurements should be taken of the item and/or location in question.

EXPERT EVIDENCE

Judges are not experts on all matters. They will often need independent experts in a particular field to provide an opinion on issues to assist them in deciding a case. The parties may also need expert evidence to help determine the strength of their case well before further costs are incurred and before proceedings are issued. For example:

- ▶ In a professional negligence action an expert may be required to give an opinion on whether the professional achieved the standard of care to be expected of a reasonably competent practitioner in all the circumstances.
- ▶ Experts may be needed to quantify the level of loss suffered in the past, or which may be suffered in the future.
- ▶ Experts may be needed to determine whether an item was defective on manufacture, supply or as a result of improper installation.

Whether an expert will be needed, the type of expert and what their qualifications should be the evidence they will need to consider, whether to appoint an expert jointly with the other parties and the timing of the expert's appointment are all things that should be considered at an early stage.

For an expert's opinion (usually in a written report, and supplemented by giving oral evidence at trial) to be admissible and given weight by the court, or accepted by the other side, it should be, and be seen to be, truly independent. A party may appoint its own independent expert to give a view on the strengths of a case before proceedings are issued, but care must be taken to ensure that the expert's independence is not compromised if it is intended to use that expert in later court proceedings.

Finalizing settlement agreements

Most disputes settle without the need to go to court, and even where proceedings have been issued most cases settle before trial. The process of resolving disputes can take up a lot of time and emotional energy, and the prospect of a settlement can be a welcome relief. Once the principal areas of agreement have been identified, parties sometimes fail to drill down into the detail required for an effective settlement. This can be for many reasons, including a fear of derailing the settlement process, or because of a desire to wrap things up as speedily as possible.

A settlement agreement which is not properly concluded or well-thought-out can lead to further problems and disputes.

ENSURE THAT SETTLEMENT NEGOTIATIONS ARE CONDUCTED AND CORRESPONDENCE MARKED 'SUBJECT TO CONTRACT' AND 'WITHOUT PREJUDICE'

Settlement negotiations may be protracted and may address different aspects of a claim at different times. Agreements can be oral or in writing. The use of the phrase **'subject to contract'** generally means that the discussions and agreements are not intended to be binding until formally recorded in a written agreement. This will assist in ensuring that there is no agreement until all the terms have been agreed and put in writing.

The **without prejudice rule** (see above) enables parties to a dispute to discuss the dispute freely and without fear that concessions made with a view to seeking a compromise are not used against them in formal proceedings.

RECORD THE SETTLEMENT AGREEMENT IN WRITING

It is possible to have a settlement agreement which is entirely oral, part oral and part in writing, or all in writing. Settlement agreements should ideally be recorded in writing to reduce the scope for disputes in the future as to what exactly had been agreed.

RECORD ALL THE TERMS OF THE AGREEMENT

The agreement should record all matters agreed. Points to consider include:

▶ *Who are the parties to the agreement?*
▶ *Will all parties to the dispute be parties to and bound by the agreement?* If not, further related claims may follow. For example, in a dispute between party A, party B and party C, if A and B settle their dispute, then (unless otherwise agreed) B will be entitled to continue a claim against C. C might then join A in the dispute between B and C, with the result that A remains exposed to claims and costs despite its settlement with B.
▶ *Does the person signing the agreement have the authority to enter into a binding agreement?* For example, an accounts clerk may not have the authority to bind his/her company to an agreement. Authority of the directors may be required, or they may need to provide evidence of any delegation of authority they have given to the person who is to sign the document.

- ▶ *Is the settlement to cover only known claims, or all claims whether known or unknown at the time of settlement?*
- ▶ *How and when is payment to be made?* Is payment to be made by instalments? What agreement is there in relation to interest – both on the primary sum claimed and in the event of late payment following settlement?
- ▶ *What is the position in relation to legal costs?* Are the parties to bear their own legal costs, or is one party to be responsible for paying the other party's costs? Is there a specific sum agreed for costs and, if not, how will the level of costs to be paid be determined?
- ▶ *Are there to be any conditions precedent to the settlement?* For example, the agreement might only become binding if and when payment is made, or documents or goods delivered.
- ▶ *Confidentiality and announcements.* Is the agreement, or parts of it, to be kept confidential? Is there to be a press statement or other announcement and, if so, in what terms?
- ▶ *Tax.* What will the tax consequences of the settlement be? Who is to bear the cost of any tax payable?

What is mediation?

- ▶ This is the process that lets parties in a dispute reach their *own settlement* or agreement, but with the help of a third person who guides and sometimes leads them to this goal.
- ▶ The mediator is *neutral* and is normally a well-trained professional.
- ▶ It is a *voluntary* process and cannot be imposed upon you, although sometimes commercial agreements provide for parties to try mediation before litigation in the courts. If you take part in mediation, you can leave at any time. This compares favourably in a sense with litigation where, once you are engaged, there are normally prohibitively expensive consequences of disengaging – you are 'dancing with a gorilla' and can only stop with the consent of the beast.
- ▶ Mediation is *confidential* both as far as the outside world is concerned and what is said to the mediator by each side in private session is treated in confidence, unless he/she is authorized to disclose.

▶ It is *informal* and *flexible*. It can be conducted by telephone or even online, over a period of days, weeks or in one session. People can stay together all the time, but it is normal for them to separate to allow the mediator to get to the heart of the matter with each side in private to encourage greater communication. These private sessions are in effect the engine room of mediation and where the mediator seeks to bring each side to the settlement zone.

▶ *It works* and in civil mediation where commercial, contractual and other disputes are dealt with, often in a day or less; over 80 per cent of disputes are settled and mostly on the day.

How is mediation practised in the UK?

HISTORY

Mediation has been used as a method of solving disputes since ancient times. But it was not until the 1990s that it began to be accepted by the mainstream legal community as a viable alternative to litigation.

Judges were given the power to suggest to parties that they should mediate, rather than proceed straight to litigation. This was to avoid potential waste of time, money and scarce public resources. With our courts overstretched, judges have begun to use this power. The government has caught onto the idea and is pushing for more cases in different sectors to be mediated rather than taken to trial. Now parties who refuse to mediate without good reason may have to pay some or all of the other side's legal costs, even if they eventually win their case.

ATTITUDES TO MEDIATION

You will find that attitudes to mediation range from the full embrace of the convert to the extreme wariness of the unbeliever. Sometimes people have had bad experiences with mediation, or know those who have. You will almost certainly come across people who will tell you that mediation is a waste of time and money and that to suggest it is a sign of weakness.

It is true that mediation is not suitable for every case and not all mediations end in settlement. However, mediation is a valuable tool that should be considered for every dispute, and understanding it is vital for any professional involved with litigation or dispute resolution. One of the most important things for a business is that early use of mediation can stop a dispute escalating and can permit preservation of commercial relationships.

COSTS OF MEDIATION

The cost of a mediation will depend on who is involved and how long it takes, as well as the worth of the dispute. If a party wants to be accompanied by his/her lawyer, or an independent expert, then the lawyer's costs need to be considered as well as the mediator's fees. You will also need to think about where the mediation will be held and what refreshments will be provided in working out the total cost. A day at mediation can cost as much as a day at trial in larger disputes. The big difference is that this is normally a one-off cost. Trial only comes after months and sometimes years of expense getting to the final hearing.

Mediators usually have an hourly and a daily fee which varies depending on their expertise. They typically charge more for mediations which run over their standard hours (usually 9.30 a.m. to 5.00 p.m.). Increasingly, though, as people become more accustomed to the process, a result can be achieved in half a day with corresponding cost saving.

An alternative method of charging that you may see is the linking of the mediator's fees to the amount of money at stake in the dispute. This can be combined with the daily/hourly fee model.

On average, a day-long mediation with just the parties and a mediator will cost between £600 and £3,000 plus VAT. It is usual for the parties to split any costs between them, although in some cases it is usual for one party to pay all the costs (e.g. the employer usually pays in employment disputes).

There are also local community organizations that offer free or cheap mediation.

As mediation is now seen as a normal part of the litigation process, it can also be available on legal aid or on legal expenses insurance (though not for business disputes in the case of legal aid).

TYPES OF MEDIATION

One of mediation's great strengths is that it is a flexible process. It can be employed for any type of dispute. It can last an hour, or a day or longer. It can be concluded in one session, or over several, with the parties together or in separate rooms. There may be one mediator (usual in commercial claims) or two co-mediators (usual in workplace or community mediation).

Mediation by telephone/online can be particularly helpful where the parties are geographically far apart because it saves on costs and travel time.

CONFIDENTIALITY

Mediation is a confidential process. The parties and the mediator usually agree to keep everything that happens in the mediation confidential.

During the mediation, you can tell as much or as little as you want to the other party. Anything you tell the mediator in confidence should be kept in confidence and he/she should check with you what can be told to the other party.

The exception to this is if the mediator thinks that there is risk of criminal action or harm to someone. These situations are extremely rare and the mediator will consider very carefully before breaking confidentiality. He/she may prefer to terminate the session rather than disclosing anything without consent.

Anything said at a mediation is usually considered 'without prejudice' and cannot be used as evidence in a court claim. There are a few, very unusual exceptions to this rule. Once an agreement is reached, 'without prejudice' usually does not apply and you will need to make sure that any settlement agreement deals explicitly with confidentiality to ensure that any confidentiality obligations are legally binding. Once the 'without prejudice' falls away, then the settlement agreement can be relied on before a court in the same way as any other agreement reached between parties.

THE PARTIES WILL REACH THEIR OWN AGREEMENT

The mediator has no authority to decide the dispute or to impose an agreement on the parties. They are not a judge or an arbitrator. The parties will decide the outcome of the mediation. Because the parties create and agree to any settlement, they are more likely to be happy with it and to stick to its terms. Asked by a party 'what do you think of that argument?', the mediator will normally reply that it is not a matter for him/her.

Benefits and disadvantages of mediation

ADVANTAGES

Flexible process, flexible outcome
Mediation is a flexible process and gives parties access to a wide range of outcomes not available in litigation. Usually, all a court will do is order one party to pay money to the other. In mediation, because the parties come to their own agreement, other things can be taken into account to address the parties' unique needs. For an example, see the case study below:

Case study

A partnership had two partners, and they had fallen out. The partners were at very different stages in their lives: one was 60 and looking forward to retirement and the other was 40 and looking forward to growing the business to reap rewards in the future.

They had received an offer to buy the business. The 60-year-old wanted to accept, but the 40-year-old did not and they were in deadlock as neither could act without the other's agreement. The 40-year-old had offered to buy out the 60-year-old, but not for a price the 60-year-old found acceptable. They thought they might have to dissolve the partnership, which would mean they both lost something into which they had put a lot of work and which was really valuable to them.

They agreed to attend a mediation. Despite knowing each other very well, and discussing the situation in detail, they had been unable to find a way forward. The partnership agreement was complex and a good legal outcome was not something either partner could contemplate with any certainty. At the mediation, they found a resolution which took into consideration more than the law, and the legal interpretation of their partnership agreement.

The 60-year-old agreed to take less money for his share of the business, but on condition that he was able to continue to use the prestigious offices at no cost for 18 months to do business with his best clients in order to make up the difference between the price he wanted and what his partner was prepared to pay. The 40-year-old got to pay less upfront, and a 'clean doorstep' handover for when he took over the business. They also preserved their personal and professional relationship, which was of great value to both of them.

Speed
Court proceedings can take months, or even years to reach a conclusion. Mediation can be over in a day or even hours and can be arranged at short notice. It also requires less time from parties than litigation, meaning that parties can be freed up to concentrate on their business and administrative day-to-day concerns.

Economic
Mediation fees will nearly always be far lower than the costs of litigation. Of course, if the mediation does not result in a settlement, then the mediation fees will be in addition to any litigation costs. However, the mediation process usually increases the parties' understanding of each other and the claims. This can be very helpful in the litigation or in promoting settlement later.

Certainty within the parties' control
In court, the decision is up to a judge, a tribunal or a jury. The outcome of any litigation is uncertain up to the point where a judgment is given and, even then, that judgment may be the subject of an appeal by the losing side. And that is before arguments about costs. A mediation in which an agreement is reached gives parties certainty on the day, in an outcome that they control.

Suited to assessing complex issues
Mediation can be conducted with significant input from experts, a specialist mediator (e.g. someone who is an expert and a mediator) or the parties themselves. This makes the process ideal for examining and allowing the parties to assess complex issues together in a way that is not possible in litigation.

Preserves relationships
Mediation preserves relationships and can even make them stronger. Unlike more adversarial processes, because mediation encourages

parties to look for mutual solutions they are more likely to discover mutual interests. They are also more likely to achieve an understanding of each other's needs and businesses. This can lead to very beneficial and long-lasting relationships emerging from a dispute.

Examples of this include business relationships (e.g. where colleagues or partners have left a business after a dispute, but on resolution of the dispute continue to help each other via referrals and with ongoing cases) and personal relationships (e.g. neighbours or spouses who, after resolution of the dispute, help each other with childcare and community issues).

Can address all issues
Mediation can address all the issues that concern the parties, not just the legal points or the financial issues. This can be very effective in disputes where people's emotions are involved, due to the cathartic nature of the process. Acknowledgement and apology (both unlikely in litigation!) can go a long way to resolving a dispute. We find this is true for commercial/business disputes as well as for disputes that are traditionally considered 'emotional' such as divorces or discrimination claims.

For an example of how expressing emotion can clear the air even in a business dispute, see the case study above.

DISADVANTAGES

Additional costs if unsuccessful
If the mediation does not result in a settlement, then the costs will be in addition to any litigation costs. However, the mediation process usually increases the parties' understanding of each other and the claims and this can be very helpful in the litigation or in promoting settlement later.

Voluntary and non-binding process
Mediation is a non-binding process, though many mediations end with a legally binding settlement agreement. It is a voluntary process and requires both parties to want to mediate. A party cannot be forced to take part in a mediation like a defendant is forced to take part in litigation. There is nothing (other than common sense!) to prevent a party withdrawing partway through a mediation if they wish to do so.

Fishing expeditions

Occasionally, someone will come to a mediation to attempt to extract useful information from the other party, rather than with the desire to reach an agreement. An experienced mediator can usually spot this and may call a halt to the mediation. Mediations are usually confidential and without prejudice, but will involve giving some information about your position to the other party. Of course, this works both ways, so if you are on a fishing expedition – beware! We have seen the fisher caught, and those who intended a fishing expedition ending up with a settlement because of what they discovered.

Fishing expeditions and Part 36 offers

One particular trick we have seen is a party attending a mediation and then using the information they get about the value of the claim to make a **Part 36 offer**. A Part 36 offer is a formal offer than can affect how much of the other side's (and your own) legal costs you have to pay, depending on the outcome of the litigation. Where this tactic is used, it is usually to put pressure on the other side to accept a low settlement offer.

However, planned exploitation of what was learned at a mediation to make a Part 36 offer is unusual, and, like any fishing expedition tactic, can backfire!

Does not stop legal deadlines

Mediation does not halt the litigation process. It will not affect your legal deadlines. If you need more time to try mediation before a deadline (such as a hearing), you need to apply to the court or tribunal and ask them to grant you an extension of time or to stay (suspend) the proceedings. It is important that all litigation deadlines are met, unless you have permission from the court to extend them.

Mediation is not an easy option

While mediation can be easier than a court hearing, it can also be very intense. It is important that you do not underestimate the pressure of the process.

Mediation will not provide a precedent

A mediation settlement will not provide a precedent like a legal ruling. If you have a series of claims on similar issues, a legal ruling which sets a precedent might be valuable to you – providing, of course, that the precedent is in your favour!

No judgment, no day in court

Sometimes people want a decision by a judge about their claim. Sometimes they want their day in court, or publicity for their claim. Mediation will not give a judgment on who was right and who was wrong and its purpose is to avoid the day in court.

Seen as weakness

Some people (mistakenly) see an offer to mediate as a sign of weakness. Thankfully, this attitude is becoming less common and can usually be dealt with by explaining the benefits of mediation and emphasizing the strengths of your legal case.

Why does mediation work?

There are a number of reasons and the idea of having a sensible and competent neutral help makes it an effective tool. Singling one factor out:

Pressure-cooker effect

Mediations are usually scheduled to run for a fixed time. The process has its own momentum, which a good mediator will encourage. Most people, having spent some dedicated time trying to reach an agreement, will be reluctant to walk away without one. It is amazing how many mediations settle in the last half-hour.

In contrast, many attempts at direct settlement drag on between letters or emails and even face-to-face meetings with setbacks likely to lead to a widening of gaps. The mediator is constantly trying to narrow the gap and uses techniques and skills to do this. The mediator is a turbocharged negotiator.

Mediation providers

You do not have to go through a mediation provider, but can go directly to a known mediator. Many mediations are arranged this way and some excellent mediators work for themselves, rather than under the banner of any particular provider.

Below we have listed a few (very few) of the mediation providers available in the UK. While we have worked with some of them, we have not worked with all of them and we do not give any guarantee as to their suitability to handle your or your client's specific issues. It is important that you find a mediator with whom you or your client are comfortable.

- ▶ ADR Group
- ▶ Bevans Solicitors
- ▶ In Place of Strife
- ▶ LawWorks
- ▶ Littleton Chambers
- ▶ The Academy of Experts
- ▶ The Centre for Effective Dispute Resolution
- ▶ Clerksroom
- ▶ The TCM Group

TEST YOURSELF

1 **A breach of contract claim must be brought...**

   (a) within six years of the breach of contract

   (b) within six years of suffering loss from the breach of contract

   (c) within 12 years of the contract being formed

   (d) when you get round to it

2 **Anything said on a 'without prejudice' basis...**

   (a) is exempt from immunity of action

   (b) cannot normally be used later in legal proceedings

   (c) is confidential so you can say what you like

   (d) is normally intended to prejudice the other side greatly

3 **There is no 'property' in a witness means that...**

   (a) all witnesses in court cases do not own houses

   (b) either party may approach a potential witness and ask them to give evidence to support their case

   (c) you can slip a gold watch into their pocket to help jog their memory

4 **Mediation is...**

   (a) a compulsory part of the court process that you must complete before issuing a court claim

   (b) a voluntary process involving a neutral third party that may assist to resolve a dispute

   (c) a voluntary process where the mediator decides the dispute for the parties

   (d) a form of relaxation which may involve transcendental hallucinogenic out-of-body experiences – rather like reading this book

9

Other legal pitfalls

In this chapter you will learn about:
- **the Bribery Act 2010**
- **insolvency, both corporate and individual**
- **distance selling.**

Introduction

In this final chapter we will look briefly at other areas that could prove problematic for a business. Unfortunately, there are simply too many potential traps for this publication to provide complete coverage.

The Bribery Act 2010

The Bribery Act 2010 came into force in July 2011, making it illegal to give, promise or accept a bribe. As bribery is a criminal offence, directors, partners and managers of businesses involved can face up to ten years in jail, together with unlimited fines. Because the Act introduces bribery as a corporate offence, it means that liability rests with companies, partnerships, public sector bodies and not-for-profit organizations, as well as the individuals involved.

A corporate body has a defence if it can show that it had in place adequate procedures designed to prevent persons associated with the business from undertaking conduct which amounts to bribery. A business will therefore need to ensure that it has such procedures in place, and a good starting point is for the business to implement a policy on bribery. The government guidance indicates that what is adequate will be measured against six core principles, which are:

proportionate procedures, top-level commitment, risk assessment, due diligence, communication (including training), and monitoring and review.

Insolvency

This can affect a business in a number of direct and indirect ways. The obvious direct impact is where a business is insolvent and either it can no longer pay its debts as they fall due or it has a negative balance sheet (i.e. the liabilities are greater than the assets). It is very important, especially in a limited company, that any potential insolvency issues are identified at an early stage because, if a company is insolvent and it continues to trade at a time when the directors knew or ought to have known that the business could not avoid insolvency, then the directors may be personally liable for any debts incurred. This blows a coach and horses through the concept of limited liability protection and could have very severe consequences for directors.

Insolvency can affect a business indirectly if, for example, customers or clients or suppliers become insolvent.

There are different types of insolvency proceedings and a detailed analysis is outside the scope of this book. For a limited company, the key forms of insolvency are:

► **Administration**
  ▷ In administration, a company is protected from creditors enforcing their debts while an administrator (a qualified insolvency practitioner) takes over the management of the company's trading and affairs. The administrator operates the company with a view to reorganizing it, or selling some or all of its business or assets.
  ▷ In some cases, a deal to sell the company's business and assets is negotiated before the administrator is appointed and completed immediately on appointment. This is called a pre-packaged administration sale ('pre-pack').
► **Liquidation** This is a procedure by which the assets of a company are placed under the control of a liquidator (a qualified insolvency practitioner). In most cases, a company in liquidation ceases to trade, and the liquidator will sell the company's assets and then distribute the proceeds to creditors.

► **Company voluntary arrangement (CVA)**   A CVA is an agreement between a company and its creditors by which the company compromises its debts or agrees an arrangement for their discharge. If the necessary majority of creditors approves the CVA at a creditors' meeting, then the CVA will bind all creditors (except those with security over the company's assets).

► **Receivership**   The holder of security over a company's assets may appoint a receiver to sell the assets in question and pay the proceeds to the charge-holder in satisfaction of the secured debt.

For an individual, he/she is insolvent if he/she has insufficient assets to meet their debts and liabilities. The main types of personal insolvency proceedings are:

► **Bankruptcy**
  ▷ Bankruptcy is a process, which is commenced by court order, to realize and distribute an insolvent individual's assets among his/her creditors.
  ▷ Any insolvent individual may apply to the court for his/her own bankruptcy. Alternatively, a creditor may issue a bankruptcy petition against an insolvent individual.
  ▷ After an individual is made bankrupt, a trustee in bankruptcy is appointed. All the assets in the individual's 'bankruptcy estate' vest in the trustee, and the ability of a bankrupt individual to trade and take credit is restricted.
  ▷ An individual's bankruptcy usually lasts for one year, although the realization and distribution of assets by his/her trustee in bankruptcy may take longer.

► **Individual voluntary arrangement (IVA)**
  ▷ An IVA is an agreement between an insolvent individual and his/her creditors which either compromises his/her debts, or provides a framework for their settlement.
  ▷ Any insolvent individual may propose an IVA to his/her creditors and also has the option of seeking a court order preventing creditors taking recovery action in respect of their debts until they have voted on the IVA proposal.
  ▷ An IVA comes into force if more than 75 per cent (by value) of those creditors attending the creditors' meeting, to consider the proposal, vote in favour of it. When an IVA

comes into effect, it binds all creditors who were entitled to be notified of the IVA proposals, even if they voted against the IVA or did not, in fact, receive notice of the proposals.

Distance selling

If goods are sold to consumers by mobile phone, email, website, telephone, fax or interactive television, sellers must comply with the Distance Selling Regulations.

There are four main obligations on suppliers of goods and services by distance means. They are:

1 To provide upfront information to consumers before the contract is concluded.
2 To provide certain information to consumers before the delivery of the goods or supply of the services requested.
3 To commit to delivering the goods and/or services within 30 days.
4 To provide a seven-(working)-day cooling-off period, during which consumers can withdraw from the contract without penalty and without giving a reason. The only charge that can be made to consumers for exercising their rights is the direct cost of returning the goods. If the trader does not give consumers details about their right to cancel the contract, the period is extended from seven days to three months.

There are certain exceptions to the rules, such as the supply of products that, by their nature, may not be returned (such as perishable food) or bespoke products.

The Data Protection Act

The Data Protection Act applies whenever an organization uses personal data. Data is defined in the Act as being where information:

a is being processed by means of equipment operating automatically in response to instructions given for that purpose
b is recorded with the intention that it should be processed by means of such equipment

c is recorded as part of a relevant filing system or with the intention that it should form part of a relevant filing system

d does not fall within paragraphs (a), (b) or (c) but forms part of an accessible record as defined by section 68, *or*

e is recorded information held by a public authority and does not fall within any of paragraphs (a) to (d).

'Relevant filing system' is defined and has been the subject of case law. The Information Commissioner regards a relevant filing system as being:

> *...intended to cover non-automated records that are structured in a way which allows ready access to information about individuals. As a broad rule, we consider that a relevant filing system exists where records relating to individuals (such as personnel records) are held in a sufficiently systematic, structured way as to allow ready access to specific information about those individuals.*

If your organization is dealing with data, then the next issue is whether it is **personal data**:

Personal data means data which relates to a living individual who can be identified:

1 from that data, *or,*

2 from that data and other information which is in the possession of, or is likely to come into the possession of, the data controller, *and*

3 includes any expression of opinion about the individual and any indication of the intentions of the data controller or any other person in respect of the individual.

There is also a further category of **sensitive personal data** to which additional safeguards are applied:

Sensitive personal data means personal data consisting of information as to:

1 the racial or ethnic origin of the data subject

2 his/her political opinions

3 his/her religious beliefs or other beliefs of a similar nature

The Data Protection Act will apply whenever a business is processing personal data. This covers obtaining, recording or holding the information or data or carrying out any operation or set of operations on the information or data, including:

▶ organization, adaptation or alteration of the information or data

▶ retrieval, consultation or use of the information or data

▶ disclosure of the information or data by transmission, dissemination or otherwise making available, *or*

▶ alignment, combination, blocking, erasure or destruction of the information or data.

The Act then goes on to list out eight key obligations when processing personal data:

1 Personal data shall be processed fairly and lawfully and, in particular, shall not be processed unless certain conditions are met which vary depending on whether you are processing personal data or sensitive personal data.

2 Personal data shall be obtained only for one or more specified and lawful purposes, and shall not be further processed in any manner incompatible with that purpose or those purposes.

3 Personal data shall be adequate, relevant and not excessive in relation to the purpose or purposes for which they are processed.

4 Personal data shall be accurate and, where necessary, kept up to date.

5 Personal data processed for any purpose or purposes shall not be kept for longer than is necessary for that purpose or those purposes.

6 Personal data shall be processed in accordance with the rights of data subjects under this Act.

> **7** Appropriate technical and organizational measures shall be taken against unauthorized or unlawful processing of personal data and against accidental loss or destruction of, or damage to, personal data.
>
> **8** Personal data shall not be transferred to a country or territory outside the European Economic Area unless that country or territory ensures an adequate level of protection for the rights and freedoms of data subjects in relation to the processing of personal data.

The Information Commissioner has summarized the eight key principles as follows:

FIRST PRINCIPLE

In practice, it means that you must:

- ► have legitimate grounds for collecting and using the personal data
- ► not use the data in ways that have unjustified adverse effects on the individuals concerned
- ► be transparent about how you intend to use the data, and give individuals appropriate privacy notices when collecting their personal data
- ► handle people's personal data only in ways they would reasonably expect, *and*
- ► make sure you do not do anything unlawful with the data.

SECOND PRINCIPLE

In practice, the second data protection principle means that you must:

- ► be clear from the outset about why you are collecting personal data and what you intend to do with it
- ► comply with the Act's fair processing requirements – including the duty to give privacy notices to individuals when collecting their personal data
- ► comply with what the Act says about notifying the Information Commissioner, *and*
- ► ensure that, if you wish to use or disclose the personal data for any purpose that is additional to or different from the originally specified purpose, the new use or disclosure is fair.

THIRD PRINCIPLE

In practice, this means you should ensure that:

► you hold personal data about an individual that is sufficient for the purpose you are holding it for in relation to that individual, *and*

► you do not hold more information than you need for that purpose.

FOURTH PRINCIPLE

To comply with these provisions you should:

► take reasonable steps to ensure the accuracy of any personal data you obtain

► ensure that the source of any personal data is clear

► carefully consider any challenges to the accuracy of information, *and*

► consider whether it is necessary to update the information.

FIFTH PRINCIPLE

In practice, it means that you will need to:

► review the length of time you keep personal data

► consider the purpose or purposes you hold the information for in deciding whether (and for how long) to retain it

► securely delete information that is no longer needed for this purpose or these purposes, *and*

► update, archive or securely delete information if it goes out of date.

SIXTH PRINCIPLE

The rights of individuals that it refers to are:

► a right of access to a copy of the information comprised in their personal data

► a right to object to processing that is likely to cause or is causing damage or distress

► a right to prevent processing for direct marketing

► a right to object to decisions being taken by automated means

► a right in certain circumstances to have inaccurate personal data rectified, blocked, erased or destroyed, *and*

► a right to claim compensation for damages caused by a breach of the Act.

The most commonly invoked right is for an individual to make a subject access request. This must be done in writing and the organization can insist that a fee of £10 is paid. An individual is entitled to be told whether any personal data is being processed; given a description of the personal data, the reasons it is being processed, and whether it will be given to any other organizations or people; given a copy of the information comprising the data; and given details of the source of the data (where this is available).

In most cases you must respond to a subject access request promptly and in any event within 40 calendar days of receiving it.

SEVENTH PRINCIPLE

In practice, this means you must have appropriate security to prevent the personal data you hold being accidentally or deliberately compromised. In particular, you will need to:

- ▶ design and organize your security to fit the nature of the personal data you hold and the harm that may result from a security breach
- ▶ be clear about who in your organization is responsible for ensuring information security
- ▶ make sure you have the right physical and technical security, backed up by robust policies and procedures and reliable, well-trained staff, *and*
- ▶ be ready to respond to any breach of security swiftly and effectively.

EIGHTH PRINCIPLE

This one is fairly self-evident.

TEST YOURSELF

1 Bribery is...

   (a) a necessary part of any arms deal

   (b) something to turn a blind eye to

   (c) an offence for which the person who offered a bribe can be punished

   (d) an offence for which the person who offered a bribe as well as the corporate body for whom they work can be punished

2 A company continues to trade at a time when the directors knew or ought to have known that the business could not avoid insolvency. The effect of this is that...

   (a) the company incurs greater debts and can be fined

   (b) the directors can be held personally responsible for the debts incurred

   (c) some poor sod loses out but not the directors who simply start up a new business

3 If your business supplies goods via the Internet, then the Distance Selling Regulations...

   (a) provide that the goods must be dispatched within 14 days of the order

   (b) allow the customer a seven-day cooling-off period during which they may cancel the order

   (c) mean that the customer must live at least 30 miles away from you

4 The Data Protection Act applies...

   (a) only to sensitive and confidential information

   (b) only if the business turnover is greater than £2 million

   (c) whenever a business processes data

   (d) only if it suits

Annex 1: Sample employment contract

You should take independent legal advice before using this document.

THIS AGREEMENT IS MADE ON [DATE]

BETWEEN

EMPLOYER of [ADDRESS] ('Company or we')

AND

EMPLOYEE of [ADDRESS]

Commencement of employment

1.1 Your employment with the Company commenced on [DATE]. [No employment with a previous employer counts towards your period of continuous employment with the Company **OR** Your employment with [NAME], which commenced on [DATE], counts towards your period of continuous employment with the Company].

1.2 The first [NUMBER] month[s] of your employment shall be a probationary period and your employment may be terminated during this period at any time on [one week's] prior notice. We may, at our discretion, extend this period for up to a further [NUMBER] months. During this probationary period your performance and suitability for continued employment will be monitored. [At the end of your probationary period you will be informed in writing if you have successfully completed your probationary period.]

Job title

2.1 You are employed as [JOB TITLE]. [Your duties are set out in the attached job description.]

2.2 You may be required to undertake other duties from time to time as we may reasonably require.

2.3 You warrant that you are entitled to work in the UK without any additional approvals and will notify the Company immediately if you cease to be so entitled at any time during your employment with the Company.

2.4 You shall not work for anyone else while you are employed by the Company unless we have consented in writing.

Place of work

3.1 Your normal place of work is [LOCATION] or such other place as we may reasonably determine.

Salary

4.1 Your [basic] salary is £[AMOUNT] per year which shall accrue from day to day and be payable [monthly] in arrears [on or about the [DATE] of each month] directly in to your bank or building society account.

4.2 We shall be entitled to deduct from your salary or other payments due to you any money which you may owe to the Company at any time.

Hours of work and rules

5.1 Your normal hours of work are between [TIME] and [TIME] [Mondays] to [Fridays] inclusive with a lunch break of one hour. You may be required to work such additional hours as may be necessary for the proper performance of your duties without payment for overtime.

5.2 You are required at all times to comply with our rules, policies and procedures in force from time to time [including those contained in the Staff Handbook, [a copy of which has been given to you **OR** which is available from [POSITION] **OR** which is available on our intranet. The Staff Handbook is/is not contractual]].

Holidays

6.1 You are entitled to [NUMBER] days' holiday during each holiday year. In addition you are entitled to take the usual public holidays in England and Wales [or a day in lieu where we require you to work on a public holiday]. You will be paid your normal basic remuneration during such holidays. The Company's holiday year runs between [DATE] and [DATE]. If your employment starts or finishes part way through the holiday year, your holiday entitlement during that year shall be calculated on a pro-rata basis.

6.2 You shall give at least [NUMBER] weeks' notice of any proposed holiday dates and these must be agreed by [POSITION] in writing in advance. [No more than [NUMBER] days' holiday may be taken at any one time unless prior consent is obtained from [POSITION].] We may require you to take holiday on specific days as notified to you.

6.3 You cannot carry [more than [NUMBER] days of] untaken holiday entitlement forward from one holiday year to the following holiday year.

We shall not pay you in lieu of untaken holiday except on termination of employment. The amount of such payment in lieu shall be 1/26oth of your salary for each untaken day of holiday.

If you have taken more holiday than your accrued entitlement at the date your employment terminates, we shall be entitled to deduct from any payments due to you one day's pay calculated at 1/26oth of your salary for each excess day.

Sickness absence

7.1 If you are absent from work for any reason, you must notify [POSITION] of the reason for your absence as soon as possible but no later than [TIME] on the first day of absence.

7.2 In all cases of absence a self-certification form, which is available [on the Company's intranet **OR** from [POSITION]], must be completed on your return to work and supplied to [POSITION]. For any period of incapacity due to sickness or injury which lasts for seven consecutive days or more, a doctor's certificate stating the reason for absence must be obtained at your own cost and supplied to [POSITION]. Further certificates must be obtained if the absence continues for longer than the period of the original certificate.

7.3 You agree to consent to a medical examination (at our expense) by a doctor nominated by the Company should the Company so require. You agree that any report produced in connection with any such examination may be disclosed to the Company and the Company may discuss the contents of the report with the relevant doctor.

7.4 If you are absent from work we shall pay you:

Statutory Sick Pay (**SSP**) provided that you satisfy the relevant requirements[; and Company sick pay in accordance with the provisions of clause o, provided that you comply with our procedures regarding sick leave [and the Company's sick pay policy]].

Your qualifying days for SSP purposes are [Monday] to [Friday].

7.5 [Once you have completed [NUMBER] month[s] continuous service with the Company you will be entitled to receive payment for periods of absence during any consecutive 12-month period from the first day of absence on the following basis:

[SET OUT SICK PAY PROVISIONS IF ANY] up to a maximum of [NUMBER] [days **OR** weeks **OR** months] in any 12-month period.]

7.6 [We reserve the right to withhold payment of Company sick pay if you fail to comply with the provisions of clause o and clause o.].

Termination and notice period

8.1 After successful completion of your probationary period as provided in clause o, and subject to clause o, the prior written notice required from you or the Company to terminate your employment shall be as follows:

> one [calendar month's] prior written notice until you have been continuously employed for four complete years; and
> one additional week's notice for each completed year of continuous employment thereafter up to a maximum of 12 weeks' notice.

We shall be entitled to dismiss you at any time without notice [or payment in lieu of notice] if you commit a serious breach of your obligations as an employee, or if you cease to be entitled to work in the United Kingdom.

Disciplinary and grievance procedures

9.1 Your attention is drawn to the disciplinary and grievance procedures applicable to your employment, which are [contained in the Staff Handbook **OR** available from [POSITION]]. These procedures do not form part of your contract of employment.

9.2 If you wish to appeal against a disciplinary decision you may apply in writing to [POSITION] in accordance with our disciplinary procedure.

9.3 We reserve the right to suspend you with pay for the purposes of investigating any allegation of misconduct or neglect against you.

9.4 If you wish to raise a grievance you may apply in writing to [POSITION] in accordance with our grievance procedure.

Pensions

10.1 [There is no entitlement to pensions benefit in relation to your employment, however the Company shall provide access to a designated stakeholder pension scheme as required by law. The Company does not make any contributions to such stakeholder scheme.

OR

You are entitled to become a member of the [NAME] Pension Scheme, subject to satisfying certain eligibility criteria and subject to the rules of such scheme as amended from time to time. Full details of the scheme are available from [POSITION].]

10.2 A contracting-out certificate is [not] in force in respect of your employment.

Collective agreement

[There is no collective agreement which directly affects your employment.

OR

The collective agreement between [NAME] and [NAME] dated [DATE], a copy of which [you have been given **OR** is available from [POSITION]], directly affects your employment.]

Changes to your terms of employment

12.1 We reserve the right to make changes to any of your terms of employment. You will be notified in writing of any change as soon as possible and in any event within one month of the change.

Confidential information

13.1 You shall not use or disclose to any person either during or at any time after your employment with the Company any confidential information about the business or affairs of the Company [or any of its business contacts], or about any other matters which may come to your knowledge in the course of your employment. For the purposes of this clause o, **confidential information** means any information or matter which is not in the public domain and which relates to the affairs of the Company [or any of its business contacts].

13.2 The restriction in clause o does not apply to:

prevent you from making a protected disclosure within the meaning of section 43A of the Employment Rights Act 1996; or
use or disclosure that has been authorized by the Company, is required by law or by your employment.

Company property

14.1 All documents, manuals, hardware and software provided for your use by the Company, and any data or documents (including copies) produced, maintained or stored on the Company's computer systems or other electronic equipment (including mobile phones), remain the property of the Company.

14.2 Any Company property in your possession and any original or copy documents obtained by you in the course of your employment shall be returned to [POSITION] at any time on request and in any event prior to the termination of your employment with the Company.

Third party rights

15.1 No person other than you and the Company may enforce any terms of this agreement.

Signed for and on behalf of the Company

....

Signed by the Employee

....

Answers to Test yourself sections
(we thought we said no cheating)

Chapter 1

1 = False, 2 = (a), 3 = (b), 4 = (a), 5 = (b), 6 = False, 7 = (a)

Chapter 2

1 = (a), 2 = (b) and (c), 3 = (a), 4 = (a)

Chapter 3

1 = True, 2 = (b), 3 = False, 4 = (a), 5 = (c)

Chapter 4

1 = (d), 2 = (b), 3 = (a), 4 = (b), 5 = (c), 6 = (a), (b) and (c), 7 = (b), 8 = (a) or (b), although (a) is quicker and, with less than a year's service, carries little risk of any future claim

Chapter 5

1 = False – the terms are set out only after the contract has been formed and performed, 2 = (c), 3 = False, 4 = (b)

Chapter 6

1 = (b), 2 = (a), 3 = True, 4 = (a)

Chapter 7

1 = (a) possibly but definitely (b) and (c), 2 = (b), 3 = (a)

Chapter 8

1 = (b), 2 = (b), 3 = (b), 4 = (b)

Chapter 9

1 = (d), 2 = (b), 3 = (b), 4 = (c)

Index